Cherish and Relish

Everyday Indian Vegetarian and Non-Vegetarian Recipes

Nawabzadi Fatima Alam Khan

Acknowledgements

Nawab Mir Usman Alam Khan, Nawab of Belha and Surat (Dad)
Kulsum Begum, Begum of Belha and Surat (Mom)
Nawabzada Mir Maqbool Alam Khan (Brother)
Nawabzadi Zehra Batul Alam Khan (Sister)
Syed Mohommed Quadry (Husband)
Zahara Quadry (Daughter)
Zoha Quadry (Daughter)

Photography : Nawabzadi Fatima Alam Khan
                       Syed Mohommed Quadry

Author : Nawabzadi Fatima Alam Khan

Picture on the front cover : Butter Chicken *(page 28)*

Picture on the back cover : Vegetable Stew *(page 54)*

Video Recipes : www.cherishandrelish.com

First Edition : April 2016

ISBN Paperback: 978-0-9938424-2-9

ISBN Hardback: 978-0-9938424-0-5

© Fatima 2016

WORLD COPYRIGHTS RESERVED. All rights reserved. All recipes, photographs and drawings are original and copyrighted. No part of this book may be reproduced in any form including, but not limited to, storage in a retrieval system or transmission in any form or by any means, electronic, mechanical, photocopied, scanned, downloaded, recorded, or otherwise, without prior written permission of the author and the publisher.
While every precaution is taken in the preparation of this recipe book, the publisher and the author assume no responsibility for errors or omissions. Neither is any liability assumed for damages resulting from the use of the information contained herein.

INTRODUCTION

I have had a dream – indeed, an abiding passion – for the past 25 years to write a cookbook. I began my journey of writing and collecting recipes at 13 and to this day I cherish this interest. The end result is this labour of love that I wish to share with all lovers of good food.

This book is a combination of recipes that have been passed on to me by my mother and recipes that I have tried to perfect along the way. My parents, the Nawab and Begum of Belha and Surat, have always been appreciative of good food that fed both body and soul. The cuisine at home was Hyderabadi-influenced from my mother's side and Surti and Mughlai from my father's. Not surprisingly, those royal influences are reflected in many of the recipes listed in this book.

My husband and I have clicked all the photographs included in this book. All the recipes contained in this book are kitchen tested. I have thoroughly enjoyed every moment of conceptualizing this recipe book and, at the same time, my family has enormously enjoyed all the dishes in this book.

Some of the recipes in this book have played center stage at many festivals, cultural events and special occasions that my family has celebrated. We have savoured, relished and cherished these recipes. The book encompasses dishes such as mutton biryani and sheer korma that are traditionally served on festivals as well as recipes that are part of our daily cuisine such as coconut chicken curry, bagharay baingan, kaali daal, tomato egg curry and fried fish masala.

At a time when the opportunities of having family get-togethers are becoming increasingly rare, it becomes all the more important to make these occasions memorable. The anticipation, excitement and sheer joy of cooking up a feast has the ability to unite and enrich our souls.

This book is a result of my personal culinary journey and also provides an opportunity for everyone to get in the kitchen and cook up a dish to enjoy and a story to appreciate. I hope you are inspired by each page to cook up your own story.

Nawabzadi Fatima Alam Khan

CONTENTS

NON-VEGETARIAN STARTERS
8 Shami Kebab *(Minced Meat Cutlets)*
9 Fried Chicken
10 Mutton Chops
11 Aloo Kheema Cutlets *(Potato Minced Lamb Cutlets)*
12 Fried Chicken Sandwich
13 Chicken Spring Roll
14 Steamed Kheema Kebabs *(Steamed Lamb Mince Cutlets)*
15 Meatloaf

VEGETARIAN STARTERS
16 Cauliflower Soup
17 Bread Aloo Pakoda *(Bread Potato Dumplings)*
18 Dahi Vada *(Fried Lentil Savoury Dumplings)*
19 Cauliflower Pakodas *(Cauliflower Fritters)*
20 Aloo Baingan Cutlets *(Potatoes Stuffed with Brinjal Cutlets)*
21 Egg Mayonnaise Sandwich
22 Vegetable Sandwich with Green Chutney
23 Onion Fritters

NON-VEGETARIAN MAIN COURSE DISHES
CHICKEN DISHES
24 Khada Masala Chicken *(Chicken Cooked With Whole Spices)*
25 Coconut Chicken Curry
26 Cashew Chicken
27 Chicken Masala Curry
28 Butter Chicken
29 Nargisi Kofta Curry *(Boiled Eggs Wrapped In Lamb / Chicken Mince)*
30 Tandoori Chicken
31 Green Chicken Curry

LAMB DISHES
32 Kacche Gosht Ke Kofte *(Meatballs With Gravy)*
33 Kali Mirchi Ka Gosht *(Peppered Lamb)*
34 Paaya *(Trotters)*
35 Kheema Masala *(Spiced Lamb Mince)*
36 Tomato Mutton Curry
37 Aloo Gosht ka Salan *(Potato Lamb Curry)*
38 Baked Kheema *(Baked Lamb Mince)*
39 Lamb Roast

SEAFOOD DISHES
40 Baked Ginger Fish
41 Fried Fish Masala
42 Shrimp Coconut Curry
43 Steamed Fish Parcels
44 Khatte Theekha Jhingah *(Spicy Lemon Prawns)*
45 Cold Fish
46 Salmon with Spinach
47 Machhli ka Hara Salan *(Green Fish Curry)*

VEGETARIAN MAIN COURSE DISHES
48 Masala Dal *(Lentil Curry)*
49 Bagharay Baingan *(Brinjals / Eggplants In Peanut Curry)*
50 Palak Paneer *(Indian Cottage Cheese With Spinach)*
51 Tomato Egg Curry
52 Potato Rosti
53 Rai Ke Aloo *(Potatoes Tempered With Mustard Seeds)*
54 Vegetable Stew
55 Cabbage with Coconut
56 Aloo Mutter Curry *(Potato Peas Curry)*
57 Cauliflower Curry
58 Chana Masala *(Chickpea Curry)*
59 Dal Makhani *(Black Gram Lentils With Butter)*

RICE DISHES
NON-VEGETARIAN
60 Kheema Biryani *(Minced Lamb Rice)*
61 Mutton Biryani *(Lamb Rice)*
62 Chicken Biryani *(Chicken Rice)*
63 Fish Biryani *(Fish Rice)*

VEGETARIAN
64 Vegetable Pulao *(Mixed Vegetable Rice)*
65 Qubooli Pulao *(Lentil Rice)*
66 Rajma Pulao *(Kidney Bean Rice)*
67 Corn Pulao *(Corn Rice)*

RAITAS
68 Tomato Onion Raita *(Tomato Onion Mixed With Yogurt)*
68 Brinjal Raita *(Brinjals Mixed With Yogurt)*
69 Cucumber Raita *(Cucumber Mixed With Yogurt)*
69 Aloo Raita *(Potatoes Mixed With Yogurt)*
70 Okra Raita *(Okra Mixed With Yogurt)*
70 Boondi Raita *(Fried Chickpea Balls Mixed With Yogurt)*

DESSERTS
71 Mawa Cupcakes *(Indian Milk Cake)*
71 Strawberry Lemon Cheese Cake
72 Sheer Korma *(Sweetened Milk With Vermicelli)*
72 Pineapple Upside Down Cake
73 Malpua *(Sweet Indian Pancakes)*
73 Instant Kesar Kulfi *(Indian Ice- Cream Flavoured With Saffron)*

74 **GLOSSARY**
75 **KITCHEN CONVERSION TABLE**

NON-VEGETARIAN STARTERS

SHAMI KEBABS
Minced Meat Cutlets
(Makes approx. 18-20)

Ingredients

Boneless Lamb Meat – 1 kg or 2.2 lb
Chana Dal – ¾ cup (soaked for 40 mins)
Cinnamon Stick (Dalchini) - 1 (3 Inch)
Whole Cloves (Laung) - 4
Whole Cardamom (Elaichi) - 4 pods
Whole Peppercorns (Kali Mirchi) – 1 tsp
Whole Green Chillies (Hari Mirchi) - 3
Whole Red Chillies (Lal Mirchi) - 2
Garlic Paste – 2 tbsp
Ginger Paste – 2 tbsp
Onion – 1 big size (approx. 250 gms)
Mint Leaves (Pudina) – 1 bunch chopped
Coriander Leaves (Kotmir) – 1 bunch chopped
Cumin Seeds – 2 tsp
Coriander Seeds – 2 tsp
Oil – 2 tbsp (this oil will be added while boiling the meat)
Oil – as required for shallow frying the kebabs
Salt to taste

Method

1) Wash and soak the chana dal in water for 40 mins before cooking it with the meat.
2) Discard the water from the chana dal and keep it aside after it's soaked.
3) Boil the meat with all ingredients including the soaked chana dal and 2 tbsp of oil. Add 3 cups water to the meat. Cover the pot with a lid and cook on medium heat until all the water runs dry. The meat should be left dry once it's cooked. Keep stirring if required. May take approximately 2-3 hours.
4) When the meat is tender and cooked completely, discard the cinnamon stick, cardamom pods and cloves. Run the cooked meat in the blender to make into kebab consistency paste. Mix well. Now add the chopped mint leaves and coriander leaves and mix well.
5) Shape into a ball and then flatten into a round patty.
6) Heat oil in a shallow pan for 2-3 mins. Shallow fry the kebabs till brown on each side.
7) Serve shami kebabs with raita.

NON-VEGETARIAN STARTERS

FRIED CHICKEN
(Makes 8)

Ingredients

Chicken – 1 kg or 8 pieces
Ginger and Garlic Paste – 2 tbsp
Red Chilly Powder (Lal Mirchi) – ½ tsp
Cumin Powder (Zeera Powder) – 1 tsp
Pepper Powder (Kali Mirchi) – ½ tsp
Salt to taste
Oil – 2 tbsp (this oil will be added while boiling the chicken)
Oil – as required for deep frying the chicken
Chickpea Powder (Besan) or Bread Crumbs as required

Egg Batter Ingredients
Eggs – 4 or 5
Pepper Powder – ½ tsp
Salt to taste

Method
1) Boil the chicken with ginger and garlic paste, red chilly powder, cumin powder, salt and 2 tbsp of oil. Add enough water to cover the chicken pieces. Cover the cooking pot with a lid. Cook on low-medium flame.
2) Cook the chicken till tender. The water in the chicken should dry off. Remove the chicken pieces from the cooking pot. Keep the chicken pieces aside to cool on a plate.
3) In another bowl beat the eggs with pepper powder and salt.
4) Place some chickpea powder or breadcrumbs on a plate.
5) Coat each chicken piece with chickpea powder/breadcrumbs and dip it in the egg batter.
6) Deep fry the chicken pieces till medium brown.
7) Serve fried chicken pieces with raita and naans.

NON-VEGETARIAN STARTERS

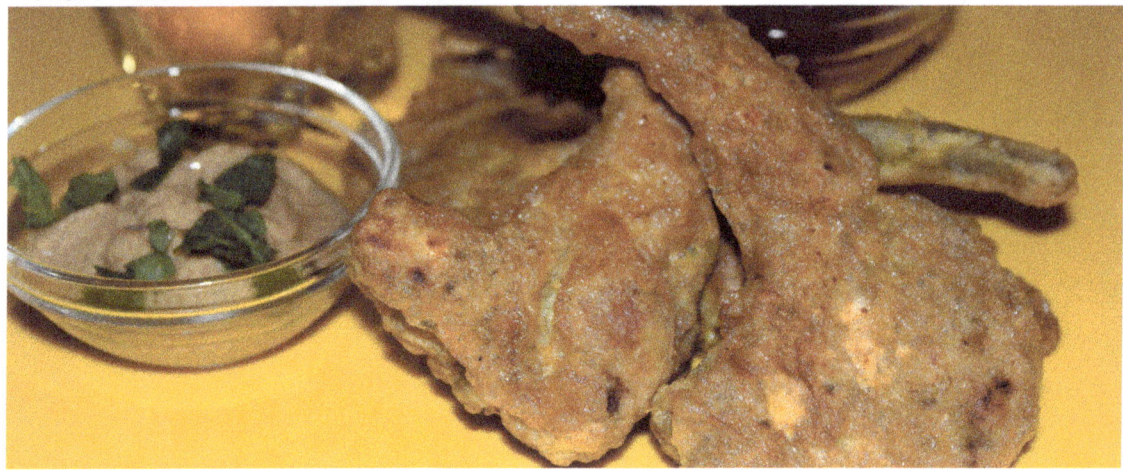

MUTTON CHOPS
(Makes 10)

Ingredients

Mutton Chops – 10 pieces
Tomatoes – 3 big (blend them to make tomato juice)
Ginger and Garlic Paste – 2 tbsp
Red Chilly Powder (Lal Mirchi) – 1 tsp
Coriander Powder (Dhania) – 1 tsp
Turmeric Powder (Haldi) – ½ tsp
Bread Crumbs / Chickpea Powder as required
Salt to taste
Oil – 2 tbsp (this oil will be added while boiling the chops)
Oil – as required for deep frying the chops
Water – 1 cup

Egg Batter Ingredients
Eggs – 4 or 5
Pepper Powder – ½ tsp
Salt to taste

Method
1) Wash and pat dry the chops.
2) Boil the mutton chops with tomato juice, ginger and garlic paste, red chilly powder, coriander powder, turmeric powder, salt and oil 2 tbsp. Add 1 cup water. Add salt when the chops are 80% cooked.
3) When the mutton chops are tender, dry off the water stirring carefully to avoid burning of the masala (spices). Cool the chops.
4) In another bowl beat the eggs with pepper powder and salt.
5) Heat oil in a pan for deep frying the chops.
6) Roll the chops in breadcrumbs or chickpea powder and then dip them in the egg batter and deep fry till medium brown.
7) Mutton chops are ready to serve with raita and naans.

ALOO KHEEMA CUTLETS
(Potato Minced Lamb Cutlets)
(Makes approx. 6-7 cutlets)

Ingredients

Filling Ingredients
Lamb Mince – ½ kg
Onion – 1 small finely chopped
Red Chilly Powder (Lal Mirchi) – ½ tsp
Ginger and Garlic Paste – 1 tbsp
Cumin Powder (Zeera) – 1 tsp
Garam Masala Powder – 1 tsp
Turmeric Powder (Haldi) – 1 tsp
Cinnamon Stick (Dalchini) – 1 (3 inch)
Whole Cardamom (Elaichi) – 3 pods
Pepper Powder – ½ tsp (optional)
Salt to taste
Oil as required

Potato Preparation Ingredients
Potatoes (Aloo) – 5 big
Salt to taste

Method
Lamb Mince
1) Fry the finely chopped onions in 2 tbsp oil. After the onions turn translucent add red chilly powder, ginger and garlic paste, cumin powder, garam masala powder, turmeric powder, cinnamon stick, cardamom, salt and pepper. Sauté well for 1 min.
2) Add the minced lamb and cook the lamb in it's own water. Add 1 cup water only after the original water of lamb mince has evaporated. Let the lamb mince cook till done. Discard the cinnamon stick and cardamom pods. Keep the lamb mince aside and let cool.

Potato
1) Boil the potatoes with their skin on until tender. If using the pressure cooker wait till 3-4 whistles go off. Cool the potatoes and peel the skin off.
2) Mash the peeled potatoes. Add salt to taste.

Final Method
1) Shape the mashed potato into rounds and make a well in the center. Fill in the lamb mince. Carefully close the well and shape the potato into a round. Flatten the potato cutlet between the palms.
2) In a shallow pan add some oil and fry the potato lamb minced stuffed cutlets till light golden brown. Aloo kheema cutlets / potato lamb cutlets are ready to relish.

NON-VEGETARIAN STARTERS

FRIED CHICKEN SANDWICH
(Makes approx. 6-8)

Ingredients

Boneless Chicken Breast – 2 (cubed small)
Garlic Cloves – 2 chopped finely
Spring Onions – 1 bunch (optional)
Pepper Powder to taste or ¼ tsp
Salt to taste
Butter – 125 gms
Soya Sauce – ½ tsp (optional)
Green Chillies – 1 finely chopped (optional)
Cabbage – ¼ cup finely chopped (optional)
Carrots – ¼ cup shredded (optional)
White Bread Slices – ½ to 1 loaf (use as required)
Chickpea Powder (Besan)– Use as required to make a batter with egg
Eggs – 2
Oil as required for deep frying

Method

1) Chop the chicken into very small cubes.
2) In a pan add butter and chopped garlic. Now add the cubed chicken and cook on a low flame in 1 cup water. Cook till chicken is tender. Add salt and pepper.
3) Add the finely chopped spring onions and the rest of the vegetables and cook for 10 mins or less.
4) In a bowl beat the eggs with salt and pepper powder. Add the chickpea powder to make a pancake consistency batter.
5) Trim the edges of the bread slices. Butter the slices on only one side and cut into triangular shape.
6) Place the cooked chicken on the buttered side of the triangular bread slice and make a sandwich.
7) Now dip this chicken sandwich in the chickpea egg batter. Deep fry till medium brown.
8) Fried chicken sandwich is ready to relish.

NON-VEGETARIAN STARTERS

CHICKEN SPRING ROLLS
(Makes approx. 20)

Ingredients

Boneless Chicken Breast – 2 (cubed small)
Garlic Cloves – 1 chopped finely
Spring Onions – 1 bunch
Pepper Powder to taste or ¼ tsp
Salt to taste
Soya Sauce – ½ tsp (optional)
Green Chillies – 1 finely chopped (optional)
Cabbage – ¼ cup finely chopped (optional)
Carrots – ¼ cup shredded (optional)
Spring Roll Sheets – 20 large or as required
All-Purpose Flour (Maida) – ¼ cup
Oil as required

Method

1) Heat 2 tbsp oil in a pan for 1 min. Add chopped garlic. Now add the cubed chicken and cook on low flame with 1 cup water. Once the chicken is tender, add soy sauce, pepper and salt to taste.
2) Add the finely chopped spring onions and the rest of the vegetables and cook for 10 mins or less.
3) Cover the spring roll sheets with a moist kitchen towel to avoid the sheets from drying off.
4) In a bowl add little water to the all-purpose flour to make a thick paste. This will be used to glue the edges of the spring rolls.
5) Place 1 tbsp of cooked chicken or as required on a spring roll sheet. Start rolling by folding the sheet to the center point tight. Add the all-purpose flour paste around the edges which is used as glue to seal the spring rolls.
6) In a deep pan, heat oil add the spring rolls and deep fry till golden brown.
7) Serve hot with tomato sauce.

NON-VEGETARIAN STARTERS

STEAMED KHEEMA KEBABS
Steamed Lamb Mince Cutlets
(Makes approx. 12- 15)

Ingredients

Lamb Mince or Chicken Mince – 1 kg
Onion – 1 small chopped finely
Green Chillies – 1 finely chopped (optional)
Ginger Paste – 1 tsp
Garlic Paste – 2 tsp
Red Chilly Powder – ½ tsp
Cumin Powder – 1 tsp
Coriander Powder – ½ tsp
Chicken Masala Powder or Mutton Masala Powder – ½ tsp (optional)
Coriander Leaves (Kotmir) – 1 bunch chopped finely
Mint Leaves (Pudina) – 1 bunch chopped finely
Chickpea Powder (Besan) – 1 tbsp or 1 Egg
Pepper – ½ tsp (optional)
Yogurt – 1 tbsp (optional)
Oil – 1 tbsp (optional)
Salt to taste

Method

1) In a bowl add the chopped onions and all the remaining ingredients.
2) Shape into kebabs lengthwise.
3) In a non-stick pan add oil which is optional. Now place the kebabs and let it steam in it's own water for 10-15 mins. Keep the pan covered and cook on low-medium flame.
4) Steamed lamb mince kebabs are ready to serve.

NON-VEGETARIAN STARTERS

MEATLOAF
(Serves 3)

Ingredients

Lamb Mince or Chicken Mince – 700 gms
Egg – 1 small
Onion – 2 tbsp
Chicken Stock Cube – 1 crumbled
Coriander Leaves – ½ bunch
Mint Leaves – ½ bunch
White Bread – 2 slices
Pepper Powder – ¼ tsp
Salt - a pinch since the chicken stock cube contains salt
Butter – 1 tsp

Method

1) Preheat the oven to 180ºC (350ºF).
2) Chop the edges of the bread slices. Place the bread slices in a bowl and add enough water to soak. Leave to stand for 5 mins, then drain and squeeze well to get rid of all the water.
3) Combine the bread and all the other ingredients in a bowl. Shape into a loaf then place in a tray or in an ovenproof dish. Place the meatloaf in the oven and bake for 30-45 mins until the mince is cooked.
4) Serve with mashed potatoes and salad.

VEGETARIAN STARTERS

CAULIFLOWER SOUP
(Makes 6-8)

Ingredients

Cauliflower – 1 medium or 750 gms
Vegetable Stock Cubes - 2
Heavy Cream – 1 litre
Pepper to taste
Salt to taste
Water – 1 litre

Method
1) In a pot boil chopped cauliflower florets in 1 litre of water.
2) When the cauliflower is tender take half a cup of the boiling water into a separate cup. Add the vegetable stock cubes to the hot water and pour it back into the cauliflower.
3) Now add 1 litre of heavy cream with salt and pepper.
4) Simmer for 10 mins till all is cooked well.
5) Serve hot.

VEGETARIAN STARTERS

BREAD ALOO PAKODAS
Bread Potato Dumplings
(Makes approx. 10)

Ingredients

Potatoes – 4 big
Coriander Leaves (Kotmir) – 1 bunch
Mint Leaves (Pudina) – 1 bunch
Onion – 1 finely chopped
Mustard Seeds – ½ tsp
Green Chillies – 1 finely chopped
Lemon Juice – ½ tsp
White Bread Slices – 10 approx.
Salt to taste
Water
Oil – 1 tsp and extra for deep frying the pakodas (dumplings)

Method
1) Boil the potatoes with skin on till tender. Peel and mash the potatoes. To this add chopped coriander leaves, chopped mint, chopped onions and salt.
2) In a small frying pan add 1 tsp oil. When the oil is hot add mustard seeds. As soon as the mustard seeds crackle turn off the flame. Pour this over the mashed potatoes.
3) Trim the edges of the bread slices.
4) In another large bowl add water with salt. This water is used for dipping the trimmed bread slices one at a time.
5) Dip one bread slice in the salted water and squeeze the water out. The bread slice is placed between the palms and the water is squeezed from the bread slice.
6) Shape the potatoes into a ball and wrap the potato ball with the wet bread slice sealing it.
7) In a deep frying pan add oil. In hot oil add the wrapped bread potato ball and fry till the outer covering turns light brown.
8) Serve hot with tomato sauce or mint chutney.

VEGETARIAN STARTERS

DAHI VADA
Fried Lentil Savory Dumplings
(Serves approx. 10-12)

Ingredients

Urad Dal (White Gram Lentils) – 1 cup
Moong Dal (Split Yellow Gram Lentils) – 1 cup
Red Chilly Powder – ½ tsp
Cumin Seeds – ½ tsp
Soda Bicarbonate – ½ tsp
Salt to taste
Sugar to taste
Yogurt – 500 gms
Oil as required for deep frying and tempering

Method
1) Soak both the lentils separately overnight.
2) Make a paste of the soaked lentils (dals) with salt, ¼ tsp red chilly powder in a blender. Add the soda bicarbonate. Add 2-3 tbsp water if required while blending the lentils.
3) After blending keep stirring. Scoop the upper layers of the batter and deep fry in oil till golden brown. A tablespoon can be used to shape the vadas (dumplings).
4) Now dip the fried vadas (dumplings) in salt water for 3-5 min. Squeeze the water out from the vadas.
5) Place the soft vadas (dumplings) in a dish.
6) Blend the yogurt with sugar and salt. Pour the yogurt over the fried vadas (dumplings).
7) Heat 1 tsp oil in a pan for tempering the vadas. Add cumin seeds and fry for 30 sec. Remove from the flame and add the ¼ tsp red chilly powder immediately. Pour this over the vadas.
8) Dahi vadas are ready to serve.

VEGETARIAN STARTERS

CAULIFLOWER PAKODAS
Cauliflower Fritters
(Serves approx. 4)

Ingredients

Cauliflower – 1 medium or 750 gms
Gram Flour (Besan) – 1 cup
Cumin Seeds – 1 tsp
Red Chilly Powder – ½ tsp
Coriander Leaves – 1 small bunch
Baking Powder – 1 tsp
Salt to taste
Oil for deep frying

Method
1) Mix the dry ingredients.
2) To prepare the batter add water to the dry ingredients. Add enough water to obtain a thick dropping consistency (like a pancake mix). Avoid the batter getting too thin
3) Cut the cauliflower into florets and keep aside.
4) To the batter add cauliflower florets, chopped coriander leaves, cumin seeds, and red chilly powder. Mix well.
5) Deep fry the fritters in batches in hot oil, dropping small tablespoon full of the mixture into hot oil, turning once, till golden brown.
6) Serve hot with chutney or tomato sauce.

VEGETARIAN STARTERS

ALOO BAINGAN CUTLETS
Potato Stuffed with Brinjal Cutlets
(Makes approx. 8)

Ingredients

Filling Ingredients
Brinjals – 1 big
Red Chilly Powder (Lal Mirchi) – ½ tsp
Cumin Powder (Zeera) – 1 tsp
Garam Masala Powder – ½ tsp
Turmeric Powder (Haldi) – 1 tsp
Lemon Juice – ½ tsp
Coriander Leaves – ¼ bunch chopped
Salt to taste
Oil as required

Potato Preparation
Potatoes (Aloo) – 4 big
Pepper to taste
Salt to taste

Method
1) Slice the brinjals and place them in salt water to avoid it from turning black. Shallow fry the slices of the brinjals and keep aside.
2) To the fried brinjals add red chilly powder, cumin powder, garam masala powder, turmeric powder, lemon juice and chopped coriander leaves.
3) Boil the potatoes with skin on. If using the pressure cooker wait till 3-4 whistles go off. Cool the potatoes and peel.
4) Mash the peeled potatoes. Add salt and pepper to taste.

Final Method
1) Shape the mashed potato into rounds and make a well in the center. Fill in the fried brinjals. Carefully close the well and shape the potato into a round. Flatten the potato cutlet between the palms.
2) In a shallow pan add some oil and fry the potato brinjal stuffed cutlets till light golden brown. Yummy cutlets are ready to serve with raita.

VEGETARIAN STARTERS

EGG MAYONNAISE SANDWICH
(Makes 3)

Ingredients

Eggs- 3 hard boiled
Lettuce Leaves - 3
Mayonnaise – 2 tbsp
Mustard – 1 tsp (optional)
Cream Cheese – 1 tbsp (optional)
Pepper Powder as required
Butter or Margarine Spread
Salt to taste
Bread Slices - 6

Method
1) Make hard boiled eggs. Once the eggs are boiled, let it cool for 10-15 mins. Crack the eggs gently with a spoon and remove the shell. Slice the hard boiled eggs into halves.
2) In a bowl mix the hard boiled eggs, mayonnaise, mustard, cheese, salt, pepper and one teaspoon of butter.
3) Spread some butter or margarine on a slice of bread. Spread the egg mayonnaise mixture. Add a lettuce leaf. Top with another slice of buttered bread slice. Cut the sandwich diagonally if desired before serving.

Tip: *To store the sandwiches wrap each sandwich with a cling wrap all around to preserve the freshness.*

VEGETARIAN STARTERS

VEGETABLE SANDWICH WITH GREEN CHUTNEY
(Makes 2)

Ingredients

Bread Slices – as required
Potato – 1 medium boiled and peeled
Cucumber – 2 small – (optional)
Tomatoes – 1

Green Chutney
Mint Leaves – 1 bunch
Cilantro Leaves – 2 bunch
Green Chillies – 4
Fresh Ginger – 1 inch
Lemon Juice – 2 medium
Sugar – 2 tsps
Cumin Seeds (Zeera) – 1 tsp
Chaat Masala – 1 tsp
Salt to taste
Butter or Margarine – 100 gms

Method
1) To prepare the green chutney blend the mint leaves, cilantro leaves, green chillies, ginger, lemon juice, cumin seeds, chaat masala and salt.
2) Slice the peeled boiled potatoes, cucumbers and tomatoes.
3) Butter each slice of bread and spread the green chutney over this. Place the sliced potatoes, cucumber and tomatoes over this. Top with another buttered slice of bread.
4) Vegetable sandwiches are ready to relish.

VEGETARIAN STARTERS

PYAAZ KE PAKODAS
Onion Fritters
(Makes approx. 12)

Ingredients

Gram Flour (Besan) – 1 cup
Cumin Seeds – 1 tsp
Red Chilly Powder – ½ tsp
Onion – 1 large chopped
Coriander Leaves – 1 small bunch chopped
Salt to taste
Oil for deep frying

Method
1) Mix the dry ingredients.
2) To prepare the batter add water to the dry ingredients. Add enough water to obtain a thick dropping consistency (like a pancake mix). Avoid the batter getting too thin.
3) To the batter add chopped onions, chopped coriander leaves, cumin seeds, and red chilly powder. Mix well.
4) Deep fry the fritters in batches in hot oil, dropping small tablespoon full of the mixture, turning once, till golden brown. Drain on kitchen paper. Serve hot with chutney or tomato sauce.

Tip: *Onions could be substituted with thinly sliced peeled potatoes, spinach leaves or cottage cheese.*

NON-VEGETARIAN MAIN COURSE DISHES

KHADA MASALA CHICKEN
Chicken Cooked With Whole Spices
(Serves approx. 4-6)

Ingredients

Chicken – 1 kg or 8 pieces
Onion – 1 big chopped
Small Onions – 2
Peppercorns – 2 tsp
Cinnamon Stick (Dalchini) - 1 (3 inch)
Whole Cardamom (Elaichi) – 4 pods
Whole Cloves (Laung) – 4
Whole Red Chillies – 2
Ginger Piece – 1 inch piece
Garlic Cloves - 8
Whole Garlic Bulb – 1 medium
Whole Cumin Seeds (Zeera) – 2 tbsp
Salt to taste
Oil

Method

1) Shallow fry the big chopped onion in 1 tbsp oil until translucent. Blend into an onion paste with garlic cloves and keep aside.
2) Sauté the chicken pieces in 2-3 tbsp oil.
3) Add the cinnamon stick, cardamom pods, cloves and red chillies with salt. Sauté till all water from the chicken dries off.
4) Add 2 small onions, ginger piece and garlic bulb to the above mix. Add 4-5 cups water and cook.
5) In a muslin cloth or cheese cloth place the whole cumin seeds and peppercorn seeds and tie the cheese cloth/muslin cloth into a knot. Dip this in the above chicken. Keep the pan covered. Cook on low flame for 15-20 mins or till the chicken is tender
6) Squeeze the juices from the garlic bulb and remove from the chicken curry. Remove the whole ginger piece, small onions and the muslin cloth. Place the muslin cloth in a tea strainer and press the muslin cloth with a spoon to squeeze the juices. Stir the chicken carefully incorporating all the juices.
7) Khada Masala Chicken is ready.

NON-VEGETARIAN MAIN COURSE DISHES

COCONUT CHICKEN CURRY
(Serves approx. 4-6)

Ingredients

Chicken – 1 kg or 8 pieces
Onion – 1 big sliced
Tomatoes – 2 medium (blended)
Coconut Milk – 1 cup
Garlic Paste – 2 tbsp
Red Chilly Powder – ½ tsp
Cumin Powder (Zeera) – 1 tsp
Coriander Powder (Dhania) – ½ tsp
Curry Leaves – 8 leaves
Coriander Leaves – ½ bunch chopped
Salt to taste
Oil

Method

1) Fry the onions till light pink. Make a paste of the fried onions in the blender. Add the garlic paste, cumin powder, coriander powder and chilly powder. Blend once more.
2) In the same pot that was used for frying onions, add the blended onion paste. Sauté for a minute. Add the chicken pieces and stir well till the original water of the chicken dries off. Now add salt.
3) Add the blended tomato till the oil starts to float.
4) Add the coconut milk. Add an additional 1 cup of water.
5) Add the finely chopped curry leaves and coriander leaves to the chicken.
6) Cook the chicken on low flame for 15-20 mins or till tender.
7) Serve hot with dinner rolls or rice.

NON-VEGETARIAN MAIN COURSE DISHES

CASHEW CHICKEN
(Serves approx. 4-6)

Ingredients

Chicken – 1 kg (cut into 8 pieces)
Onions – 2 big or 3 medium sliced
Cumin Powder (Zeera) – 1 tsp
Cashewnut Paste (Kaju) – 2 tbsp
Garlic Paste – 1 ½ tsp
Green Chilly Paste – 1 tsp or 1 ½ tsp
Cinnamon Stick (Dalchini) – 1 (3 inch)
Whole Cloves (Laung) – 4 pieces
Whole Cardamom (Elaichi) – 4 pods
Mint Leaves – ½ bunch chopped
Yogurt – ½ cup
Salt to taste
Oil

Method

1) In a pan add oil and fry onions till light pink. Make a paste of the onions in the blender.
2) Pour the onion paste back in the cooking pot. Now add the chicken pieces. Sauté till the water of the chicken dries off.
3) Add the garlic paste, green chillies paste, cumin powder, cinnamon stick, whole cardamom, whole cloves and salt. Stir well.
4) To the above add the yogurt and sauté till oil begins to float around the chicken.
5) Now finally add the cashewnut paste and the mint leaves with salt. Keep the cooking pot covered. Cook on low flame for 15-20 mins or till the chicken is tender.
6) Serve the cashew chicken curry with rice or naans.

NON-VEGETARIAN MAIN COURSE DISHES

CHICKEN MASALA CURRY
(Serves approx. 4-6)

Ingredients

Chicken – 1 kg (cut into 8 pieces)
Onions – 1 big or 2 small
Ginger Paste – 1 tsp
Garlic Paste – 2 tsp
Red Chilly Powder – ½ tsp
Cumin Powder (Zeera) – 1 tsp
Chicken Masala Powder – 1 tsp
Yogurt – ¾ cup
Butter – 1 stick or 120 gms
Coriander Leaves – ½ bunch chopped
Salt to taste

Method

1) Fry the onions till light pink in butter. Make an onion paste in the blender. Add the ginger paste, garlic paste, red chilly powder, cumin powder, chicken masala powder, yogurt and salt. Blend once more.
2) Pour the blended onion paste with the mixed spices into a bowl. To this add the chicken pieces and marinate for 2 hours.
3) In a pan add butter and place the marinated chicken. Keep the pan covered. Cook on low flame for 15-20 mins or till the chicken is tender. Garnish with chopped coriander leaves.
4) Serve the chicken masala curry with rice or bread naans.

NON-VEGETARIAN MAIN COURSE DISHES

BUTTER CHICKEN
(Serves approx. 4-6)

Ingredients

Boneless Chicken Breast – 600 gms cubed small
Ginger and Garlic Paste – 2 tbsp
Cashewnuts – 2 tbsp
Cream – ¼ cup
Tomato Ketchup – 4 tbsp
Saffron – 6 to 8 strands
Tomatoes – 3 medium cubed (150 gms each)
Small Onions - 2 finely chopped and fried
Coriander Leaves – ½ bunch
Red Chilly Powder – 2 tsp or as per taste
Turmeric Powder – ½ tsp
Coriander Powder (Dhania) – 2 ½ tsp
Salt to taste

Tempering
Whole Cloves – 4 pieces
Whole Cardamom – 5 pieces
Cumin Seeds (Zeera) – 1 tsp
Cinnamon Stick – 1 (3 inch)
Butter – 120 gms

Method
1) In a pot add the cubed boneless chicken. Add 1 cup of water and boil the chicken till it is 70% done. Keep the chicken aside once cooked.
2) Grind the cashewnuts, thick cream, onions, tomatoes and tomato ketchup into a fine paste. This makes the creamy cashewnut paste. Keep this aside.
3) In another pot melt butter add the cinnamon stick, whole cloves, whole cardamom, nutmeg, cumin seeds, saffron and chicken. Fry for 5-7 mins.
4) Add the ginger and garlic paste, red chilly powder, turmeric powder, coriander powder and salt. Add ¼ cup of water. Cook on low flame for approx. 10 mins.
5) Now add the ground creamy cashewnut paste. Add the chopped coriander leaves. Stirring occasionally cook for another 10-15 mins on low flame with the pot covered.
6) Serve hot with rice, dinner rolls or bread naans.

NON-VEGETARIAN MAIN COURSE DISHES

NARGISI KOFTA
Boiled Egg Wrapped in Minced Lamb / Chicken Mince
(Serves approx. 3-4)

Ingredients

Chicken Mince or Lamb Mince - 800 gms
Hard Boiled Eggs – 4
Chickpea Powder – 4 tbsp
Onions – 1 finely chopped
Tomatoes – 2 big blended
Turmeric Powder – ½ tsp
Red Chilly Powder – ½ tsp
Cinnamon Stick – 1 (3 inch)
Whole Cardamom – 4 pods
Whole Cloves – 4 pieces
Coriander Powder (Dhania) – 1 tbsp
Cumin Powder (Zeera) – 1 tbsp
Green Chillies – 1 finely chopped
Coriander Leaves (Kotmir) – ½ bunch chopped
Cumin Seeds (Zeera) – 1 tsp
Ginger and Garlic Paste – 2 tsp
Yogurt – ¼ cup
Oil as required for deep frying and cooking
Salt to taste

Method
Koftas (Meatballs)
1) To the mince chicken or mince lamb add ¼ tsp red chilly powder, ½ tbsp coriander powder, ½ tbsp cumin powder, chickpea powder and salt. Mix well.
2) Make hard boiled eggs. Once the eggs are boiled, let it cool for 10-15 mins. Crack the eggs gently with a spoon and remove the shell and let cool.
3) On a plastic sheet or wax paper spread a handful of chicken or lamb mince on it. Place the boiled egg over this and wrap with mince lamb or chicken. Remove the plastic sheet once the egg is wrapped with mince. Kofta is ready to fry.
4) Wet your hands and roll the kofta into an oval.
5) Deep fry the koftas in oil for 3-5 mins.
6) Keep aside and cool.

Korma (Gravy)
1) In a pan add oil. Once the oil is heated for 2 mins add cinnamon stick, whole cardamom, whole cloves, chopped onions, cumin seeds and salt. Add chopped onions and fry till light pink.
2) Blend the tomatoes into juice.
3) To the fried onions add the turmeric powder, ginger and garlic paste, ¼ tsp red chilly powder, ½ tbsp coriander powder, ½ tbsp cumin powder and the tomato juice.
4) When oil begins to float add the chopped green chillies and yogurt. Mix well. To this add little water. Cook for 3-5 mins.
5) Add the fried koftas carefully. Cover and cook for another 3-5 mins.
6) Garnish with chopped coriander leaves.

NON-VEGETARIAN MAIN COURSE DISHES

TANDOORI CHICKEN
(Serves 6)

Ingredients

Whole Chicken - 1 kg
Plain Yogurt – 1 cup
Fresh Lemon Juice or Vinegar – 2 tbsp
Garlic Paste – 1 tbsp
Ginger Paste – 2 tbsp
Cumin Powder – 1 tbsp
Coriander Powder – 1 tsp
Red Chilly Powder – 1 tsp
Garam Masala Powder – 1 tbsp
Black Pepper Powder – 1 tsp
Salt to taste or approx. 2 tsp
Turmeric Powder – 1 tbsp
Vegetable Oil, for brushing
Lemon Juice – 3 tbsp
Red Food Colouring - 2 drops (optional)
Cilantro Leaves for garnish – 1 bunch chopped
Onion, Tomato and Lemon, for garnish – 1 each sliced
White Vinegar- 1 cup

Method

1) Prick the chicken all over with a fork. Then, using a sharp knife, make gashes to allow the marinade through the chicken. Place the chicken in a large glass bowl. Dip chicken in the white vinegar for 30 mins. Remove the chicken from the vinegar after 30 mins and keep aside. Discard the vinegar.
2) In another glass bowl mix the yogurt, lemon juice, garlic paste, ginger paste, cumin powder, coriander powder, red chilly powder, garam masala powder, black pepper powder, turmeric powder, red food colouring (optional) and salt. Stir until well mixed, then pour the mixture over the chicken and rub it all over, turning the chicken several times. Cover and refrigerate 8-10 hours or overnight. Remove the chicken from the refrigerator atleast 30 mins before cooking.
3) Remove the chicken from the marinade, pressing lightly to extract excess marinade, and brush with oil.
4) Preheat the oven to 235ºC (450ºF). Place the chicken on a rack in a roasting pan, brush with oil, and bake, turning once, 35 to 40 mins until the juices run clear when the chicken is pierced near the bone with a knife.
5) Once the chicken is cooked, remove it from the oven. Shallow fry the chicken to achieve the tandoori chicken look. Garnish with fresh cilantro leaves, onions, tomatoes and lemon. Serve hot with bread naans.

NON-VEGETARIAN MAIN COURSE DISHES

GREEN CHICKEN CURRY
(Serves 4-6)

Ingredients

Chicken – 1 kg cut into 8 pieces
Onions – 2 medium finely chopped
Yogurt – 1 cup
Coriander Leaves – 1 bunch chopped
Mint Leaves – 1 bunch chopped
Green Chillies – 4
Cumin Powder – 1 tsp
Whole Cloves – 4
Whole Cardamom – 2 pods
Cinnamon Stick - 1 (3 inch)
Ginger Paste – 1 tsp
Garlic Paste – 2 tsp
Salt to taste
Oil

Method

1) Wash the chicken and prick it all over with a fork.
2) Heat the oil in a pan over medium heat. Add the finely chopped onions. Fry them till light pink.
3) Cut off the ends of the green chillies, coriander leaves and mint leaves.
4) Blend the green chillies, coriander leaves, mint leaves, fried onions and yogurt.
5) In the same pan which was used to fry the onions, add a little more oil. To the oil add whole cardamom, whole cloves and whole cinnamon. Now add the chicken pieces and saute' till the water from chicken dries off. It should take 4-6 mins.
6) To the chicken add ginger paste, garlic paste, cumin powder and salt. Stir for a minute. Add the blended mixture and stir well for 2-3 mins. Now add ½ cup of water. Cover the pan and cook till the chicken is tender. Serve hot with rice or bread naans.

NON-VEGETARIAN MAIN COURSE DISHES

KACCHE GOSHT KE KOFTE
Meatballs with Gravy
(Serves approx. 4)

Ingredients

Koftas
Minced Lamb – ½ kg
Chickpea Powder – 4 tbsp
Onion – 1 small
Fried Onion – 1 small (fried medium pink using 1 tbsp oil)
Garlic Cloves - 6
Whole Cumin Seeds
Cinnamon Stick (Dalchini) – 1 (3 inch)
Whole Cloves (Laung) – 2
Whole Cardomom (Elaichi) – 4 pods
Whole Red Chilly – 2
Whole Green Chilly – 1
Peppercorns – ½ tsp
Lemon – ½
Salt to taste

Gravy / Korma
Yogurt – 1 cup
Onion -1 big (fried till light pink and made into a paste)
Red Chilly Powder – ½ tsp
Garlic Paste – 2 tsp
Cumin Powder – 1 tsp
Cinnamon Stick – 1 (3 inch)
Whole Cardamom – 4 pods
Whole Cloves – 2 pieces
Water – ½ cup or 1 cup as required

Method
Koftas (Meatballs)
1) Make a paste of cinnamon stick, whole cumin seeds, whole cardamom, whole cloves, small onion, whole red chilly, whole green chilly and whole peppercorns.
2) To the above paste add the fried onions and lemon with salt. Mix well. Now add in the lamb mince and the chickpea powder. Mix well and shape into koftas (meatballs). Keep aside and prepare the korma (gravy).

Korma (Gravy)
1) Sauté the onions in oil with red chilly powder, garlic paste and cumin powder. Blend into a paste. Pour this back to the pan.
2) Add cinnamon stick, whole cardamom, whole cloves, yogurt and water.
3) Add salt and the koftas (meatballs), simmer on low flame. Cover and cook for 15-20 mins or till the koftas are done.
4) Serve hot with bread naans or rice.

Tip: *Substitute chickpea powder with fresh bread crumbs. To make fresh bread crumbs add 2 slices of bread in a blender and blend until crumbs form.*

NON-VEGETARIAN MAIN COURSE DISHES

KALI MIRCHI KA GOSHT
Peppered Lamb
(Serves approx. 4)

Ingredients

Lamb – 1 kg boneless diced into small cubes
Onion – 1 small chopped finely
Fenugreek Seeds – ¼ tsp (dry grind into powder)
Mustard Seeds – ¼ tsp (dry grind into powder)
Black Pepper Powder – 2 tsp
Green Chilly – 7 medium size chopped
Ginger Paste– 1 ½ tsp
Garlic Paste – 1 tsp
Garam Masala Powder – 1 tsp
Coriander Powder (Dhania) – 1 tsp
Turmeric Powder (Haldi) – ½ tsp
Cumin Powder- 2 tsp
Coriander Leaves for garnishing
Yogurt – 1 ½ tbsp
Oil as required
Salt to taste

Method

1) Heat oil in a pan add ginger and garlic paste. Add cumin powder and stir for 10 sec.
2) Add onion and fry them till slightly golden brown.
3) Add the cubed lamb and fry with onions till the lamb water dries off and the oil begins to float.
4) To the above add salt, black pepper, turmeric powder, coriander powder, fenugreek powder, mustard powder and garam masala powder. Fry these spices with lamb cubes for about 3 mins. If it is sticking to the pan sprinkle little water and continue stirring.
5) Now add yogurt, half of the green chillies and water (enough to tender the lamb cubes) and cook till tender.
6) When the meat is cooked add rest of the green chillies and keep frying till the oil separates. Take it off the pan.
7) Place the peppered lamb cubes in a dish garnished with coriander leaves.
8) Serve with bread naans or dinner rolls.

NON-VEGETARIAN MAIN COURSE DISHES

PAAYA
Trotters
(Serves approx. 2-3)

Ingredients

Paaya (Trotters) – 4 pieces
Onion – 2 big
Ginger and Garlic Paste – 2 ½ tbsp
Red Chilly Powder – 2 tsp or as required
Cumin Powder (Zeera) – 1 ½ tsp
Turmeric Powder (Haldi) – 1 tbsp
Cinnamon Stick -1 (6 inch)
Whole Cardamom – 4 pods
Whole Cloves – 4
Oil

Method

1) Boil the paaya (trotters). Use a large pressure cooker. Fill one-third of the pressure cooker with water.
2) Add one big onion, turmeric powder, cinnamon stick, whole cardamom, whole cloves in the pressure cooker and cook on medium flame. Wait till approximately 15-20 whistles or till done.
3) Remove the big onion from the cooked paaya (trotters).
4) In a pan add the second big onion and fry till medium pink. Blend this fried onion and the first onion from the paaya gravy.
5) Pour the blended onion back into the pan. Add the ginger and garlic paste, red chilly powder, cumin powder and salt. Now add the cooked paaya along with the whole cinnamon, whole cardamom and whole cloves from the gravy. Sauté this paaya mix for 5 mins. Then add the paaya water / gravy.
6) Simmer on low flame for 30 mins till all the masalas (spices) and paayas are cooked well.
7) Serve hot with bread naans or dinner rolls.

NON-VEGETARIAN MAIN COURSE DISHES

KHEEMA MASALA
Spiced Minced Lamb
(Serves approx. 4)

Ingredients

Lamb Mince – ½ kg
Onion – 1 small finely chopped
Red Chilly Powder (Lal Mirchi) – ½ tsp
Ginger and Garlic Paste – 1 tbsp
Cumin Powder (Zeera) – 1 tsp
Garam Masala Powder – 1 tsp
Turmeric Powder (Haldi) – 1tsp
Cinnamon Stick (Dalchini) – 1 (3 inch)
Whole Cardamom (Elaichi) – 3 pods
Yogurt – 2 tbsp (optional)
Pepper Powder – ½ tsp optional
Cilantro or Coriander Leaves - ½ bunch
Salt to taste
Oil as required

Method
1) Fry the finely chopped onions in oil. After the onions turn translucent add red chilly powder, ginger and garlic paste, cumin powder, garam masala powder, turmeric powder, cinnamon stick, cardamom and salt. Sauté well for 1 min.
2) Add the minced lamb and cook the lamb in it's own water. Add 1 cup water only after the original water of lamb mince has evaporated. Let the mince meat cook till done.
3) Garnish with chopped cilantro leaves or coriander leaves.
4) Masala Kheema is ready to relish.

NON-VEGETARIAN MAIN COURSE DISHES

TOMATO MUTTON CURRY
(Serves 3-5)

Ingredients

Lamb – 1 kg cubed with bones
Onion – 6 medium finely chopped
Tomatoes – 5 medium finely chopped
Garlic Paste – 2 tbsp
Ginger Paste – 1 tbsp
Red Chilly Powder – 1 tsp
Curry Leaves – 8
Salt to taste
Oil

Method

1) Wash the lamb pieces and keep aside.
2) Heat oil in a pan. Add the chopped onions and fry till light pink.
3) Add the cubed lamb pieces and sauté till the lamb water dries off.
4) Now add the garlic paste, ginger paste, red chilly powder, curry leaves and salt.
Sauté well for 2 mins.
5) Add the tomatoes and sauté till oil starts to float. Add ½ cup of water and cook the lamb on low-medium flame till tender. Serve hot with rice or bread naans.

NON-VEGETARIAN MAIN COURSE DISHES

ALOO GOSHT KA SALAN
Potato Lamb Curry
(Serves 3-5)

Ingredients

Lamb (Gosht) – 1 kg cubed with bones
Onion – 6 medium finely chopped
Potatoes (Aloo) – 4 cubed into large pieces
Yogurt – 1 cup
Garlic Paste – 2 tbsp
Ginger Paste – 1 tbsp
Red Chilly Powder – 1 tsp
Garam Masala Powder – 1 tsp
Cumin Powder – 1 tsp
Peppercorns – 1 tsp
Bayleaf - 1
Mint Leaves – ½ bunch chopped for garnishing
Salt to taste
Oil

Method
1) Wash the lamb pieces and keep aside.
2) Heat oil in a pan. Add the chopped onions and fry till light pink.
3) Add the cubed lamb pieces and sauté till the lamb water dries off.
4) Now add the garlic paste, ginger paste, red chilly powder, garam masala powder, cumin powder, peppercorns and salt. Sauté well for 2 mins.
5) Add the yogurt and sauté till oil starts to float. Add 4 cups of water. Cover the pot with a lid and cook the lamb on medium flame till ¾ done. Now add the cubed potatoes and the bayleaf. Cook the lamb with potatoes till tender.
6) Garnish the aloo gosht with mint leaves. Serve hot with rice or bread naans.

NON-VEGETARIAN MAIN COURSE DISHES

BAKED KHEEMA
Baked Lamb Mince
(Serves approx. 3-5)

Ingredients

Lamb Mince – 1 kg
Onion – 2 medium finely chopped
Garlic Paste – 2 tbsp
Ginger Paste 1 tbsp
Garam Masala Powder – 1 tsp
Red Chilly Powder – ½ tsp
Turmeric Powder – 1 tsp
Pepper Powder – ½ tsp
Yogurt – 2 tbsp
Meat Tenderizer (optional) – ½ tsp
Cilantro or Coriander Leaves – 1 bunch
Mint Leaves – 1 bunch
Green Chillies Whole – 3
Butter – 2 tbsp
Salt to taste
Oil

Method
1) Preheat the oven at 180° C (350° F).
2) Wash the lamb mince with turmeric powder.
3) Heat oil in a pan. Add the finely chopped onions. Fry till light brown.
4) Add all the ingredients to lamb mince along with the fried onions.
5) Place the lamb mixture in a baking dish. Cover the dish with aluminum foil.
6) Bake the lamb for 30–45 mins or till done.
Serve hot with bread naans or dinner rolls.

NON-VEGETARIAN MAIN COURSE DISHES

LAMB ROAST
(Serves approx. 8-10)

Ingredients

Lamb Leg – 1 large
Yogurt - 3 tbsp
Ginger Paste – 1 tbsp
Garlic Paste – 2 tbsp
Cumin Powder (Zeera) – 1 tbsp
Red Chilly Powder - 1 ½ tbsp
Garam Masala Powder – 1 tbsp
Turmeric Powder (Haldi) – ½ tbsp
Lemon Juice – 3 tbsp
Oil – 6 tbsp
Potatoes – 3 medium peeled and chopped lengthwise
Carrots – 1 chopped lengthwise
Onions – 6 medium peeled
Mixed Vegetables as per requirement
Tomatoes (optional)
Spring Onions – 2 bunches
Butter - 100 gms
Salt to taste
Aluminum Foil Sheet

Method

1) Blend the yogurt, ginger paste, garlic paste, cumin powder, red chilly powder, garam masala powder, turmeric powder, lemon juice, oil, butter and salt.
2) Make deep cuts all over the lamb leg and place in a large baking dish. Pour the above blended mix over the lamb leg. Add the chopped potatoes, chopped carrots, whole onions, mixed vegetables and spring onions. Cover the dish with aluminum foil sheet. Let the lamb marinate for 2 hours.
3) Preheat oven at 180° C (350° F). Bake the lamb leg for 2-4 hours. Or bake the lamb leg on low flame in the oven till the water in the lamb roast dries off. Increase the flame after the water dries off and bake for another 10 minutes. This dish requires checking the lamb roast every 2 hours.
4) Lamb roast is ready to serve with dinner rolls.

NON-VEGETARIAN MAIN COURSE DISHES

BAKED GINGER FISH
(Serves 5-7)

Ingredients

Salmon Fillet – 1 kg
Ginger Paste – 4 tbsp
Vinegar – 1 tbsp
Pepper Powder – 1 tsp or as required
Dill – 1 bunch
Rosemary as required
Olive Oil – 4 tbsp or as required
Salt to taste

Method
1) Wash the salmon and pat dry.
2) Make a marination of ginger paste, vinegar, pepper powder, salt and olive oil. Spread this over the salmon. Marinate for 30 mins in a baking dish.
3) Preheat oven at 180° C (350° F).
4) After marination place the dill leaves and rosemary beneath and above the salmon in the baking dish.
5) Bake uncovered for 30-40 mins. Serve hot with garlic bread.

NON-VEGETARIAN MAIN COURSE DISHES

FRIED FISH MASALA
(Serves 4)

Ingredients

Fish Fillets – 4
Red Chilly Powder – ½ tsp
Cumin Powder – 1 tsp
Coriander Powder – 1 tsp
Turmeric Powder – 1 tsp
Lemon Juice – 1 tsp
Oil – 4 tsp for the marination
Oil for shallow frying
Salt to taste

Method

1) Wash the fish fillets and pat dry.
2) In another dish prepare the marination masala for the fish with red chilly powder, cumin powder, coriander powder, turmeric powder, lemon juice and two teaspoons of oil. Mix well. Marinade the fish with this masala mix for 10 mins.
3) Heat oil in a pan. Shallow fry the marinated fish fillets for 4 mins on each side or till done.
4) Serve fried fish masala with onions and bread naans.

NON-VEGETARIAN MAIN COURSE DISHES

SHRIMP COCONUT CURRY
(Serves approx. 4-6)

Ingredients

Shrimps – 1 kg deveined and shelled
Onion – 1 big
Tomatoes – 2 medium (blended)
Coconut Milk – 1 cup
Curry Leaves – 8 to 10 leaves
Coriander – ½ bunch chopped
Garlic Paste – 2 tbsp
Red Chilly Powder – ½ tsp
Cumin Powder (Zeera) – 1 tsp
Coriander Powder (Dhania) – ½ tsp
Cumin Seeds – ½ tsp for tempering
Salt to taste
Oil

Method

1) Fry the onions till light pink. Make a paste of the fried onions in the blender. Add the garlic paste, cumin powder, coriander powder, chilly powder and salt. Blend once more.
2) Heat oil in a pot and add the shrimps. Stir well till the water from the shirmp dries off. Now add the blended onion paste. Sauté for 1 min. Add salt.
3) Add the tomato puree till the oil starts to float.
4) Add the coconut milk. Add an additional 1 cup of water.
5) Add the finely chopped curry leaves and coriander leaves to the shrimps.
6) Cook the shrimps for 15 mins or till done. Once the shrimps are cooked, temper with cumin seeds. To prepare the tempering add cumin seeds to hot oil and wait for 1 min. Switch off the flame and pour this cumin seeds along with the oil to the cooked shrimps. Keep the pot covered. Cook on low flame for 5 mins.
7) Serve hot with dinner rolls or rice.

NON-VEGETARIAN MAIN COURSE DISHES

STEAMED FISH PARCELS
(Serves 3-5)

Ingredients

Fish Fillets – 8
Onion – 1 large chopped into 4 pieces
Grated Coconut – ½ cup
Mint Leaves – 1 bunch
Cilantro or Coriander Leaves – 1 bunch chopped
Green Chillies – 6
Garlic Cloves – 10
Lemon Juice – 2 medium sized lemons
Sugar – 2 tsps
Cumin Seeds (Zeera) – 1 tbsp
Butter – 4 tbsp
Salt to taste

Method

1) Blend the mint leaves, cilantro leaves, green chillies, garlic cloves, lemon juice, cumin seeds, grated coconut, onion and salt. Make a paste. Add butter and mix well.
2) Wash the fish and pat dry.
3) Spread the prepared paste on each fillet. To make a parcel, wrap each fish fillet in aluminum foil. Fold and crimp the edges of the foil together.
4) In a steamer boil water. Place the wrapped fish fillets in the steamer. Steam for 15-20 mins or till done. Be careful when opening the aluminum foil since steam will escape immediately. Unwrap the fish fillet and serve hot with dinner rolls.

NON-VEGETARIAN MAIN COURSE DISHES

KHATTE THEEKHA JHINGAH
Spicy Lemon Prawns
(Serves 3-5)

Ingredients

Prawns – 2 cups deveined and shelled
Red Chilly Powder – 1 ½ tsp
Turmeric Powder – ½ tsp
Lime Juice – juice of 1 sour lime
Fenugreek Seeds – ½ tsp
Green Chillies – 3 chopped
Garlic Cloves – 4 or 5 crushed
Salt to taste

Method
1) Apply red chilly powder, turmeric powder, lime juice and salt to the prawns. Marinate for 5 mins.
2) Heat 2 tbsp oil in a pan. Fry the fenugreek seeds, crushed garlic cloves and green chillies.
3) When the green chillies change colour, add the marinated prawns. Add ¾ cup water. Cook till done. Serve the spicy lemon prawn hot.

NON-VEGETARIAN MAIN COURSE DISHES

COLD FISH
(Serves 3-5)

Ingredients

Whole White Fish – 1 (approx. 5 to 7 pounds)
Arrowroot Powder – 2 tbsp
Mayonnaise – 2 cups
Water – ½ cup room temperature
Water – ½ cup cold
Salt to taste

Garnish
Beetroots – thinly sliced and cut into ovals and half circles
Capsicum – cut into rings
Radish – sliced

Method
1) Wash and pat dry the fish.
2) Sprinkle fish with salt.
3) Place on a sheet of heavy aluminum foil. Fold the edges. Then pour in the ½ cup of room temperature water.
4) Wrap foil over fish. Fold and crimp edges together.
5) Place on a shallow pan and bake in an oven at 180° C (350° F) for 30 mins or until fish flakes with a fork.
6) While still warm fold back foil and pull it off.
7) Chill fish in the refrigerator.
8) When the fish has cooled, carefully transfer the flaked fish to a large serving dish.
9) Dissolve arrowroot powder in 2 tsp of water.
10) Now add the mayonnaise and stir well. Chill until syrupy. This is the white sauce.
11) Quickly spread all, but ¼ cup of sauce over cold fish. Chill the fish.
12) Now decorate the fish with the garnish ingredients like beetroots, capsicum, radish.
Dip the beetroots, capsicum and radish into the white sauce before placing them on the fish for garnishing.
13) Serve chilled.

Tip: *Arrowroot powder could be substituted with cornflour.*

NON-VEGETARIAN MAIN COURSE DISHES

SALMON WITH SPINACH
(Serves approx. 3)

Ingredients

Salmon – ½ kg cut into desired size
Garlic Cloves – 4
Fresh Spinach – 1 bunch or 1 kg well washed and chopped
Onions – 2 large sliced
Tomatoes – 4 large cut into quarters
Red Chilly Powder – ½ tsp
Cumin Powder – ½ tsp
Coriander Powder – ½ tsp
Turmeric Powder – ½ tsp
Whole Cloves– 4
Cinnamon Stick – 1 (3 inch)
Salt to taste
Oil

Method

1) Fry onions, garlic, cinnamon stick, cloves and tomatoes lightly. Now add all the spices. Add salt. Cook on a low flame for 3 mins.
2) Now add spinach. Cook for 10 mins. Add the salmon in the pan and continue cooking till it is soft enough to be eaten. Do not stir the pan, but shake gently to prevent burning and sticking.
3) Serve hot with dinner rolls.

NON-VEGETARIAN MAIN COURSE DISHES

MACHHLI KA HARA SALAN
Green Fish Curry
(Serves approx. 3-4)

Ingredients

Fish – ½ kg cut into desired size
Garlic Cloves – 8 or 9
Ginger Paste – 1 tbsp
Turmeric Powder – ¼ tsp
Coriander Leaves – 1 bunch
Dry Coconut Powder – 1 tbsp
Cumin Seeds – ¼ tsp
Fennel Seeds – ¼ tsp
Green Chillies – 4 or 5
Lemon – ½
Salt to taste
Oil

Method
1) Clean and cut the fish. Wash it and salt it. Keep aside.
2) Blend dry coconut powder, cumin seeds, fennel seeds, 5 garlic cloves, ginger, green chillies, turmeric powder and coriander leaves into a paste. Use ¼ cup water. Add juice of half a lemon.
3) Heat oil in a pan and fry 3-4 crushed garlic cloves. Add the blended coconut paste and a little water with salt. Cook till required amount of gravy is obtained.
4) Place the washed fish in the gravy which is cooking. Cook till fish is done.
5) Serve hot with lemon.

VEGETARIAN MAIN COURSE DISHES

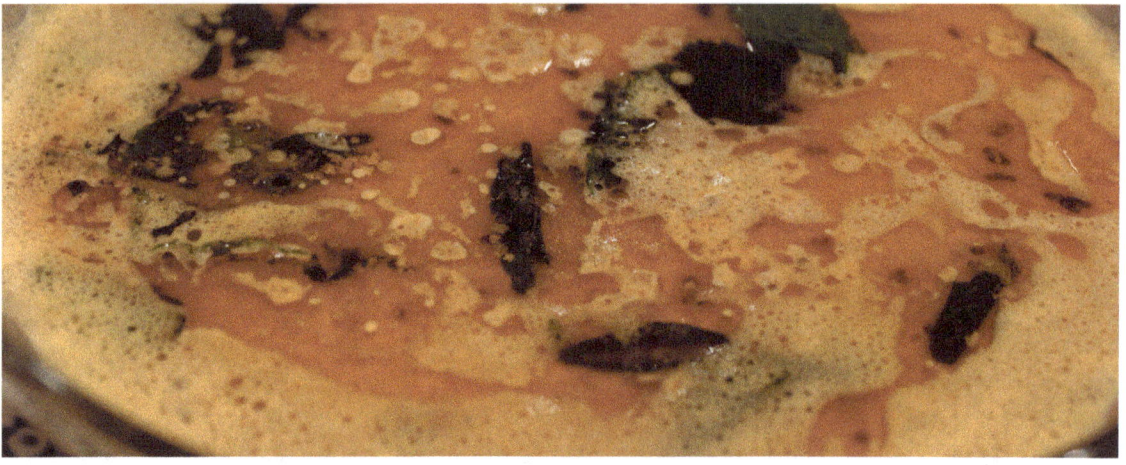

MASALA DAL
Lentil Curry
(Serves approx. 4)

Ingredients

Moong Dal (Yellow Lentil) – ¾ cup
Garlic Paste – 1 tsp
Red Chilly Powder – ½ tsp
Turmeric Powder – ½ tsp
Garam Masala Powder – 1 tsp
Mustard Seeds or Cumin Seeds – 1 tsp
Coriander Leaves – 1 bunch (optional)
Salt to taste
Oil

Method

1) Wash the lentil and soak in water for 20 mins. Drain and keep aside.
2) Now place the soaked lentils in 3 cups of water. Add garlic paste, red chilly powder, turmeric powder, garam masala powder and salt. Bring to a boil. Cook the lentils till soft. It should take approx. 15 - 20 mins. Once the lentils are done, let it cool for 15 mins.
3) Pour the lentils into a blender and blend.
4) Prepare the tempering for the masala dal. In hot oil add mustard seeds or cumin seeds and wait for 30 seconds. Switch off the flame.
5) Pour the prepared tempering over the blended lentil and immediately cover the pot with a lid. Cook the lentils for another 10 mins on low flame. Garnish the cooked lentils with chopped coriander leaves.
6) Serve hot with rice or can be relished simply as lentil soup.

VEGETARIAN MAIN COURSE DISHES

BAGHARAY BAINGAN
Brinjals (Eggplants) in Peanut Curry
(Serves approx. 3-5)

Ingredients

Brinjals – 8 small
Garlic Paste – 1 tsp
Red Chilly Powder – ½ tsp
Cumin Powder – 1 tsp
Coriander Powder – 1 tsp
Sesame Seeds – 2 tbsp
Peanuts – 4 tbsp
Onion – 2 medium
Curry Leaves – 8 or 10
Cumin Seeds – 1 tsp
Dry Coconut Powder – 4 tbsp
Cinnamon Stick – 1 (3 inch)
Tamarind – 100 gms
Green Chillies – 3 to 5 pieces
Salt to taste
Oil

Method

1) Cut the brinjals into 4 quarters leaving the stalk intact. Deep fry the brinjals 70% and keep aside.
2) Dry roast the peanuts and sesame seeds. Grind the roasted ingredients with 2 tsp water into a coarse paste.
3) In a bowl place the tamarind and add ½ cup water. Soak it for 15 mins.
4) Chop the onions. Fry them in oil. Once the onions turn translucent, remove from the pan. Grind the onions and keep aside.
5) To make the coconut milk add one cup water to the dry coconut powder. Keep aside.
5) In a bowl mix the onion paste, red chilly powder, cumin powder, coriander powder, garlic paste, peanut-sesame paste and salt. Mix well.
6) To the cooking pot add oil. Add the cumin seeds, cinnamon stick, curry leaves and chopped green chillies. Stir for 10 sec. Now add the onion paste. Sauté for 2-3 min. Add the brinjals and simmer for 3-4 mins. Add the coconut coconut milk and tamarind water. Cook for 20 mins or till done.
7) Serve hot with bread naans or dinner rolls or with biryani.

VEGETARIAN MAIN COURSE DISHES

PALAK PANEER
Indian Cottage Cheese with Spinach
(Serves approx. 3-4)

Ingredients

Spinach – 4 bunches
Indian Cottage Cheese - 300 gms cubed
Onion – 1 big finely chopped
Tomato – 1 medium finely chopped (optional)
Garlic Paste – 1 tsp
Red Chilly Powder – 1 tsp
Cumin Powder – 1 tsp
Coriander Powder – 1 tsp
Turmeric Powder – 1 tsp
Salt to taste
Oil

Method
Indian Cottage Cheese
1) Cube the cottage cheese.
2) Heat oil in a pan for deep frying the cubed cottage cheese.
3) Pour few pieces of the cubed cottage cheese and deep fry.
4) In a bowl of water add salt and keep aside. Once the cottage cheese cubes are fried pour these cubes directly into the salted water and let the cottage cheese float. After 3 mins squeeze out the water from the cottage cheese and keep aside. This method makes the cottage cheese soft and tasty.

Spinach
1) In a pot blanche the spinach leaves for 10 mins till done. Drain the water. Make a spinach paste in the blender. Keep aside.
2) In a pan heat oil. Add chopped onions and sauté. Add the garlic paste, turmeric powder, cumin powder, red chilly powder and stir for 30 sec. Now add the chopped tomato.
3) Once the oil begins to float add the blended spinach and cook for another 10 min on low flame. Add salt.
4) To the spinach add the fried cottage cheese. Cover and cook for another 5 mins on low flame.
5) Serve hot with roti or bread naans.

VEGETARIAN MAIN COURSE DISHES

TOMATO EGG CURRY
(Serves approx. 3-4)

Ingredients

Tomatoes – 15
Eggs – 3 hard boiled shelled and cut into halves
Onion – 1 big (fry the onion and make a paste)
Red Chilly Powder – 1 tsp or as per spice level
Garlic Paste – 1 tsp
Curry Leaves – 5 to 7
Cumin Seeds – 1 tsp
Oil
Salt to taste

Method

1) Heat oil in a pan. Add onions and fry till light pink. Place the fried onions into a blender and make a paste.
2) In the same pan add the cumin seeds and the onion paste. Sauté well. Now add the red chilly powder and garlic paste.
3) Add the chopped tomatoes and curry leaves. Cook till tomatoes are done or till oil begins to float in the tomato curry. Add salt now.
4) Remove the tomato curry into a serving bowl. Decorate the curry with hard boiled eggs which have been cut into halves.
5) Temper the tomato egg curry with cumin seeds. (Tempering is prepared by heating 1 tbsp oil in pan and then adding cumin seeds. Fry the seeds for 30 sec. Pour this over the tomato curry, this process is known as tempering the tomato curry).

VEGETARIAN MAIN COURSE DISHES

POTATO ROSTI
(Serves approx. 3-5)

Ingredients

Potatoes – 4 big
Onions – 2 big
Garlic Cloves – 2 chopped finely
Cheddar Cheese – 200 gms
Pepper Powder – as per taste
Salt to taste
Oil

Method
1) Peel potatoes and cut them into round slices. Deep fry and keep aside. Salt the potatoes.
2) Slice the onions into rounds. Heat oil in a pan. Add onions and chopped garlic. Fry till onions turn light pink.
3) Divide the fried onions into two portions. Keep one portion in the pan.
4) Place half of the fried potato slices over the fried onions. Spread the grated cheddar cheese over this layer. Repeat the layering with onions followed by the potatoes and finally grated cheddar cheese. Sprinkle pepper as per taste.
4) Cover the pan with a lid and cook the potato rosti till the cheese melts. Serve hot.

VEGETARIAN MAIN COURSE DISHES

RAI KE ALOO
Potatoes Tempered With Mustard Seeds
(Serves approx. 3-4)

Ingredients

Potatoes - 3 big
Garlic Paste – 1 ½ tsp
Mustard Seeds – 1 tsp
Red Chilly Powder – ½ tsp or as per spice level
Turmeric Powder – ½ tsp (optional)
Curry Leaves - 9
Green Chillies – 2 chopped (optional)
Lemon Juice – 1 tbsp (optional)
Salt to taste
Oil

Method
1) Peel and cube the potatoes. Keep aside.
2) In a pan heat oil and add mustard seeds. Wait till it crackles. Add the garlic paste, red chilly powder, turmeric powder and 1 tsp water. Stir well for 30 sec. Now add the curry leaves and the cubed potatoes with salt and lemon juice. Add the green chillies (optional). Stir for 3 mins. Now add 2 cups water and let the potatoes cook till done.
3) Serve hot with bread naans or roti.

VEGETARIAN MAIN COURSE DISHES

VEGETABLE STEW
(Serve approx. 6-8)

Ingredients

Peas – 1 cup
Yam – 1 medium
Carrots – 1 large
Sweet Potatoes – 3 large
Onions – 1 cup
Cherry Tomatoes – 8 to 10
Green Chillies – 3
Coriander Leaves – 1 bunch
Vinegar – 2 tbsp
Sugar – 1 tsp
Red Chilly Powder – 1 tsp
Salt to taste
Oil for frying all the ingredients

Method
1) Chop all onions. Fry and keep aside.
2) Cut all the vegetables into cubes and fry separately except the tomatoes, coriander leaves and green chillies. Keep the fried vegetables aside.
3) To the same oil add all the fried ingredients. Cook on low flame with salt, fried onion, sugar, vinegar, red chilly powder, chopped green chillies, chopped coriander leaves and tomatoes.
4) Cover the pot and cook till tomatoes are slightly soft.
5) Serve hot with bread naans or dinner rolls.

VEGETARIAN MAIN COURSE DISHES

CABBAGE WITH COCONUT
(Serves approx. 3-4)

Ingredients

Cabbage - 1 big size
Garlic Paste – 2 tsp
Coconut Powder – ½ cup
Fenugreek Seeds – 1 tsp
Mustard Seeds – 1 tsp
Cumin Seeds – 1 tsp
Curry Leaves – 6 to 8
Green Chillies – 4
Salt to taste
Oil

Method
1) Chop the cabbage finely. Keep aside.
2) Heat oil in a pan. Add the cumin seeds, mustard seeds, fenugreek seeds, green chillies, curry leaves and sauté for 1 min. Now add the garlic paste and stir.
3) Add the chopped cabbage and stir for 4 mins.
4) Mix ½ cup of coconut powder with ½ cup water. Pour this into the cabbage. Add salt and stir for another 4 mins on medium flame.
5) Cook the cabbage till done. Serve hot with dinner rolls.

VEGETARIAN MAIN COURSE DISHES

ALOO PEAS CURRY
Potato Peas Curry
(Serves approx. 3-5)

Ingredients

Potatoes – 4 large cubed
Peas – 1 cup
Garlic Paste – 2 tsp
Green Chilly Paste – 1tsp
Mustard Seeds – 1 tsp
Cumin Seeds – 1 tsp
Fenugreek Seeds - 1 tsp
Curry Leaves – 6
Salt to taste
Oil

Method
1) Peel and cube the potatoes. Shell the peas. Keep aside.
2) Heat oil in a pan. Add cumin seeds, mustard seeds, fenugreek seeds and curry leaves. Wait till the crackling sound of mustard is heard. Now add garlic paste and green chilly paste. Sauté for 2-3 mins.
3) Add the peas and stir for 3-4 mins. Then add the potatoes. Stir for another 4 mins. Add enough water to cover the potatoes. Cover the pan and cook on medium flame till potatoes are done.
4) Serve hot with rice or dinner rolls.

VEGETARIAN MAIN COURSE DISHES

CAULIFLOWER CURRY
(Serves approx. 3-4)

Ingredients

Cauliflower – 1 large cut into florets
Garlic Paste – 2 tsp
Green Chilly Paste – 1tsp
Mustard Seeds – 1 tsp
Cumin Seeds – 1 tsp
Fenugreek Seeds - 1 tsp
Curry Leaves – 6
Salt to taste
Oil

Method
1) Cut the cauliflower into florets. Keep aside.
2) Heat oil in a pan. Add cumin seeds, mustard seeds, fenugreek seeds and curry leaves. Wait till the crackling sound of mustard is heard. Now add garlic paste and green chilly paste. Sauté for 2-3 mins.
3) Add the cauliflower florets and stir for 3-4 mins. Add 1 cup water. Cover and cook the cauliflower on medium flame till done.
4) Serve hot with dinner rolls.

VEGETARIAN MAIN COURSE DISHES

CHANA MASALA
Chickpea Curry
(Serves approx. 3 - 4)

Ingredients

Chickpea – 1 can (540ml or 600gms)
Onions – 2 medium chopped finely
Tomatoes – 1 chopped
Coriander Leaves – ½ bunch
Garlic Paste – 2 tsp
Garam Masala Powder – 1 tsp
Red Chilly Powder – ½ tsp
Cumin Seeds – 1 tsp
Coriander Powder – ½ tsp
Cumin Powder – 1 tsp
Turmeric Powder – ½ tsp
Salt to taste
Oil

Method
1) Drain the water from the canned chickpea. Keep aside.
2) Heat oil in a pan. Add onions and fry till light golden brown.
3) Add all the spices and garlic paste. Stir for 2 mins.
4) Now add the chopped tomatoes and cook till oil begins to float. Then add the chickpeas and salt. Cover and cook for 20 mins on low flame.
5) Garnish with coriander leaves. Serve hot with bread naans.

VEGETARIAN MAIN COURSE DISHES

DAL MAKHANI
Black Gram Lentil Curry with Butter
(Serves approx. 4-6)

Ingredients

Black Gram Lentils – 1 cup
Kidney Beans (Rajma) – ½ cup soaked overnight
Onion – 1 big
Green Chillies – 2 pieces
Ginger and Garlic Paste – 1 tbsp
Tomato – 1 big (make a puree)
Garam Masala Powder – ½ tsp
Turmeric Powder – ½ tsp
Cumin Seeds for tempering – 1 tsp
Salt to taste
Oil

Method
1) Boil the black lentils, kidney beans, onion, green chillies, turmeric powder and salt till tender.
2) Add the tomato puree once the lentils are cooked. Add the ginger garlic paste and garam masala powder. Let this simmer on medium heat for 10 mins. Blend the cooked lentils once it's cooled down.
3) Temper the lentils with cumin seeds.
(Tempering is prepared by heating oil in pan and then adding cumin seeds. Fry the seeds for 30 secs. Pour this over the prepared lentils. This process is known as tempering the lentils).

RICE DISHES - NON-VEGETARIAN

KHEEMA BIRYANI
Minced Lamb Rice
(Serves approx. 3 – 5)

Ingredients

Lamb Mince – ½ kg
Onion – 1 small finely chopped
Red Chilly Powder (Lal Mirchi) – ½ tsp
Ginger and Garlic Paste – 1 tbsp
Cumin Powder (Zeera) – 1 tsp
All-Spices Powder (Garam Masala) – 1 tsp
Turmeric Powder (Haldi) – 1 tsp
Cinnamon Stick (Dalchini) – 1 (3 inch)
Whole Cardamom (Elaichi) – 3 pods
Pepper Powder – ½ tsp (optional)
Cilantro Leaves – ½ bunch chopped
Salt to taste
Oil as required

Rice

Rice – 500 gms or 2 ½ cups
Whole Cardamom – 2 pods
Cinnamon Stick – 1 (3 inch)
Whole Cloves – 2
Salt to taste
Water as required
Oil

Method
Kheema (Minced Lamb) Preparation
1) Fry the finely chopped onions in oil. After the onions turn translucent add red chilly powder, ginger and garlic paste, cumin powder, garam masala powder, turmeric powder, cinnamon stick, cardamom, pepper powder and salt. Sauté well for 1 min.
2) Add the minced lamb and cook the lamb in it's own water. Add 2 cups water only after the original water of lamb mince has evaporated.
3) Now let the lamb mince cook further till the additional water evaporates. Simmer on medium flame. Once the lamb mince is done keep it aside.

Rice Preparation
1) Wash the rice. Soak rice for 20 mins before cooking.
2) In a large cooking pot fry the onions. Add cinnamon stick, whole cloves, whole cardamom, salt and the rice. Sauté gently for 2 mins. Add 6 cups of water.
3) Cook the rice till 75% done, then strain the water from it and keep it aside.

Layering the Kheema Biryani
1) In a pot spread the cooked minced meat (kheema) as the first layer.
2) The second layer should be rice followed by the minced meat. The final layer should be rice. Spread the cilantro leaves over the topmost layer of the rice. Cover the pot with the lid and cook on medium low flame for 10 -15 mins.
3) Serve hot with raita.

RICE DISHES - NON-VEGETARIAN

MUTTON BIRYANI
Lamb Rice
(Makes for 4)

Ingredients

Mutton (with bones) – 1 kg
Rice – ½ kg or 2 ½ cups
Ginger Paste – 1 tbsp
Garlic Paste – 2 tbsp
Whole Cumin Seeds (Zeera) – 1 tsp
Oil – as required
Onions – 3 or 4 medium
Red Chilly Powder – 1 tsp
Bay Leaf (Tej Patta) – 2 (1 for the meat and 1 for the rice)
Whole Cloves – 8 (4 cloves for the meat and 4 cloves for the rice)
Whole Cardamom (Elaichi) – 8 pods (4 pods for the meat and 4 pods for the rice)
Cinnamon Stick (Dalchini) – 2 (3 inch each- 1 stick for the meat and 1 stick for the rice)
Turmeric Powder (Haldi) – 1 tsp
Sour Yogurt – ½ cup
Nutmeg (Jaiphal) – 15 gms (optional)
Mace (Javitri) – 15 gms
Mint Leaves – ½ bunch
Lemon – ½ lemon
Saffron Strands - 8 to 10 soaked in 4 tbsp of milk
Masoor Dal (optional) – ½ cup
Potatoes (optional) – 1 big
Salt to taste

Rice

Rice – 500 gms or 2 ½ cups
Whole Cardamom – 2 pods
Cinnamon Stick – 1 (3 inch)
Whole Cloves – 2
Salt to taste
Water and Oil as required

Method for Meat Preparation
1) Boil the masoor dal and keep aside.
2) Boil potatoes. Peel and cut lengthwise or cube. Shallow fry the potatoes. Keep aside.
3) In oil fry the onion brown. Add meat and stir well for 5 mins. Now add ginger paste, garlic paste, whole cumin seeds, red chilly powder, bay leaf, whole cinnamon, whole cardamom, whole cloves and turmeric powder. Add 4 cups water. Cook on low flame till meat is tender.
4) When the meat is tender add sour yogurt, nutmeg, mace, mint leaves, lemon and saffron. Cook this for 10 mins. Keep aside.

Rice Preparation for Biryani
1) Wash the rice. Soak the rice for 20 mins before cooking.
2) In a cooking pot boil 6 cups of water . Add cinnamon stick, whole cloves, whole cardamom, salt and ghee / butter or oil. Add the rice.
3) When the rice is 75% done (the rice grains begin to dance), strain it in a colander. It takes 10-15 mins for the rice to cook at the required consistency. The rice will get completely cooked once it's layered with the prepared mutton. This rice is used for layering in biryani.

Method for Layering
1) First Layer is the prepared mutton. Second layer is the prepared rice followed by the masoor dal, potatoes, pudina, saffron soaked in milk. Repeat the process till the rice becomes the topmost layer.
2) Cook the mutton biryani on low-medium flame covered with a lid for 10-15 mins or when rice is done (place a flat frying pan beneath the cooking pot to avoid the biryani from burning).
8) Serve hot with raita.

RICE DISHES - NON-VEGETARIAN

CHICKEN BIRYANI
Chicken Rice
(Serves approx. 3-5)

Ingredients

Chicken – 1 kg (cut into 10 pieces)
Onions – 3 large cut finely lengthwise
Yogurt – 1 cup
Garlic Paste – 2 tbsp
Ginger Paste – 1 tbsp
Red Chilly Powder – 1 tsp
Garam Masala Powder – 1 tsp
Cumin Powder – 1 tsp
Chicken Biryani Masala – 1 tbsp (optional)
Lemon Juice – 2 tbsp
Mint Leaves – 1 Bunch
Coriander Leaves – 1 Bunch
Saffron – 7 to 8 strands soaked in 2 tbsp milk
Salt to taste

Rice
Rice – 500 gms or 2 ½ cups
Whole Cardamom – 2 pods
Cinnamon Stick – 1 (3 inch)
Whole Cloves – 2
Salt to taste
Water as required
Oil
Bay leaf – 1 piece

Method for Chicken Preparation
1) Chop onions thinly lengthwise. Fry till light brown. The fried onion is known as "brishta". Keep half the fried onions aside and use the remaining half for marination.
2) Marinate the chicken for 1 hour with yogurt, garlic paste, ginger paste, red chilly powder, garam masala powder, cumin powder, salt and fried onions.
3) Heat oil in a cooking pot. Cook the marinated on a low flame till tender. Do not cover the cooking pot.

Rice Preparation for Biryani
1) Wash the rice. Soak the rice for 20 mins before cooking.
2) In a cooking pot boil 6 cups of water. Add cinnamon stick, whole cloves, whole cardamom, salt and ghee/butter or oil. Add the rice.
3) When the rice is 75% done (the rice grains begin to dance), strain it in a colander. It takes 10-15 mins for the rice to cook at the required consistency. The rice will get completely cooked once it's layered with the prepared chicken.
4) Layering method – First Layer is the prepared chicken. Second layer is the prepared rice followed by the onion brishta, mint leaves, coriander leaves, saffron soaked in milk. Repeat the process till the rice becomes the topmost layer.
5) Cook the chicken biryani covered for 10-15 mins or when rice is done. Place a flat frying pan beneath the cooking pot to avoid the biryani from burning.

RICE DISHES - NON-VEGETARIAN

FISH BIRYANI
Fish Rice
(Serves approx. 4-6)

Ingredients

Fish – ½ kg
Basmati Rice – ½ kg washed and soaked for 30 minutes
Onions – 3 medium sliced
Oil – 1 ½ cup
Yogurt – ½ cup beaten
Tomato – 1 medium washed and chopped
Fresh Ginger and Garlic Paste – 2 tbsp
Green Chili Paste – 1 tsp
Cinnamon Stick – 1 (3 inch)
Coriander Powder – 1 tsp
Cumin Powder – 1 tsp
Turmeric Powder – 1 tsp
Red Chili Powder – 1 tsp
Mint Leaves – 1 bunch
Coriander Leaves – 1 bunch
Salt

Marination
Lemon Juice – 2 tbsp
Red Chili Powder – 1 tbsp
Fresh Curry Leaves – 8 leaves washed and torn

Rice
Rice – 500 gms or 2 ½ cups
Whole Cardamom – 2 pods
Cinnamon Stick – 1 (3 inch)
Whole Cloves – 2
Salt to taste
Water and Oil as required

Method
1) Marinate the fish with the ingredients mentioned under "marination" for 10 mins in a dish. Keep aside.
2) Heat oil in a pan. Add sliced onion and fry until its light brown. Remove it from the oil.
3) Fry the marinated fish in the remaining oil and keep aside. Pour the remaining oil in a pan.
4) Add the ginger paste, garlic paste and green chilli paste.
5) Stir-fry for 2 mins until the oil separates from the paste.
6) Now add all the masala powder, chopped tomato and curry leaves to it. Mix well.
7) Stir in yogurt and the fried onion. Add salt to taste.
8) Cook for 5 mins, stirring continuously, on medium heat.
9) Add the fried fish, coriander and mint leaves. Keep aside.
10) Wash the rice. Soak the rice for 20 mins before cooking.
11) In a cooking pot boil 6 cups of water. Add cinnamon stick, whole cloves, whole cardamom, salt and ghee/butter or oil. Add the rice.
12) When the rice is 75% done (the rice grains begin to dance), strain it in a colander. It takes 10-15 mins for the rice to cook at the required consistency. The rice will get completely cooked once it's layered with the prepared chicken.
13) Now use a large pot and alternately arrange layers of rice and fried fish in this.
14) Cook on high flame for 5 mins. Lower flame and cook for 20 mins on very low heat.
15) Mix well and serve hot with raita.

RICE DISHES - VEGETARIAN

VEGETABLE PULAO
Mixed Vegetable Rice
(Serves approx. 4-6)

Ingredients

Potatoes – 4 medium (peeled and cut lengthwise)
Cauliflower – 1 big (broken into florets)
French Beans – ½ cup (chopped half and boiled)
Carrots – ¼ cup (chopped small and boiled)
Brinjals – 3 medium (cut into rounds)
Corn Kernels – ¼ cup (boiled)
Onions – 2 medium (fried till golden brown for the layering process)
Onion – 1 big (fried till light pink)
Yogurt – ½ cup
Ginger and Garlic Paste – 1 tbsp
Red Chilly Powder – ½ tsp or as per spice level
Cinnamon Stick – 1 (3 inch)
Whole Cardamom – 4 pods
Whole Cloves – 2
Cumin Powder (Zeera) – ½ tsp
Salt to taste
Oil
Coriander Leaves – 1 bunch
Mint Leaves – 1 bunch
Lemon - 1 (juice of 1 lemon)
Tomatoes – 2 small (chopped)
Rice – 500 gms or 2 ½ cups

Method

1) Heat oil in a pan. Add salt to avoid the oil from splashing while frying all the vegetables. Add each vegetable one at a time and deep fry. Keep it aside.
2) In the same oil fry 2 medium onions till golden brown and keep it aside. This will be used for the layering process.
3) Fry 1 big onion till light pink. Add the cinnamon stick, whole cardamom, whole cloves, ginger and garlic paste, red chilly powder and cumin powder. Stir well. Add all the boiled vegetables and sauté well.
4) Now add the chopped tomatoes and cook till oil begins to float. Now add the remaining vegetables which were deep fried. Stir well. Also add half of the coriander leaves and half of the mint leaves with lemon juice and stir well. Cook for 5 mins till all the vegetables catch the flavours of the spices.
5) Wash the rice. Soak the rice for 20 mins before cooking.
6) In a cooking pot boil 6 cups of water. Add cinnamon stick, whole cloves, whole cardamom, salt and ghee/butter or oil. Add the rice.
7) When the rice is 75% done (the rice grains begin to dance), strain it in a colander. It takes 10-15 mins for the rice to cook at the required consistency. The rice will get completely cooked once it's layered with the prepared vegetables.
8) First layer should be vegetables, followed by the coriander and mint leaves and then rice. Repeat this process 2-3 times till the rice is the topmost layer. On the final layer of the vegetable pulao spread the golden fried onions. Cover and cook on low heat for 10-15 mins.
9) Serve hot with raita.

RICE DISHES - VEGETARIAN

QUBOOLI PULAO
Lentil Rice
(Serves approx. 4-6)

Ingredients

Chana Dal (Yellow Split-Lentils) – 1 cup
Onions – 2 medium (fried till golden brown for the layering process)
Onion – 1 big (fried till light pink)
Yogurt – ½ cup
Ginger and Garlic Paste – 1 tbsp
Red Chilly Powder – ½ tsp or as per spice level
Cumin Powder (Zeera) – ½ tsp
Cinnamon Stick – 1 (3 inch)
Whole Cardamom – 4 pieces
Whole Cloves – 2 pieces
Coriander Leaves – 1 bunch
Mint Leaves – 1 bunch
Salt to taste
Oil
Lemon - 1 (juice of 1 lemon)
Tomatoes – 2 small (chopped)
Rice – 500 gms or 2 ½ cups

Method
1) Soak the lentils for 2 hrs. Discard the water from the lentils and keep aside. Boil the lentils with 6 cups of water till tender and whole.
2) In the oil fry 2 medium onions till golden brown and keep it aside. This will be used for the layering process.
3) Fry 1 big onion till light pink. Add the cinnamon stick, whole cardamom, whole cloves, ginger and garlic paste, red chilly powder and cumin powder. Stir well.
4) Now add the chopped tomatoes and cook till oil begins to float. Stir well. Also add half of the coriander leaves and half of the mint leaves with lemon juice and stir well. Cook for 2 mins till the lentils catches the flavours of the spices.
5) Wash the rice. Soak the rice for 20 mins before cooking.
6) In a cooking pot boil 6 cups of water. Add cinnamon stick, whole cloves, whole cardamom, salt and ghee/butter or oil. Add the rice.
7) When the rice is 75% done (the rice grains begin to dance), strain it in a colander. It takes 10 -15 mins for the rice to cook at the required consistency. The rice will get completely cooked once it's layered with the prepared qubooli (lentils).
8) First layer should be lentils, followed by the coriander and mint leaves and then rice. Repeat this process 2-3 times till the rice is the topmost layer. On the final layer of the qubooli pulao spread the golden fried onions. Cover and cook on low heat for 10-15 mins.
8) Serve hot with raita.

RICE DISHES - VEGETARIAN

RAJMA PULAO
Kidney Bean Rice
(Serves 4-6)

Ingredients

Kidney Beans (Rajma) – 1 can (600 gms)
Onions – 2 medium (fried till golden brown for the layering process)
Onion – 1 big (fried till light pink)
Yogurt – ½ cup
Ginger and Garlic Paste – 1 tbsp
Red Chilly Powder – ½ tsp or as per spice level
Cumin Powder (Zeera) – ½ tsp
Cinnamon Stick – 1 (3 inch)
Whole Cardamom – 4 pods
Whole Cloves – 2
Coriander Leaves – 1 bunch
Mint Leaves – 1 bunch
Lemon - 1 (juice of 1 lemon)
Tomatoes – 2 small (chopped)
Salt to taste
Oil
Rice – 500 gms or 2½ cups

Method

1) Discard the water from the kidney beans can.
2) In the oil fry 2 medium onions till golden brown and keep it aside. This will be used for the layering process.
3) Fry 1 big onion till light pink. Add the cinnamon stick, whole cardamom, whole cloves, ginger and garlic paste, red chilly powder and cumin powder. Stir well. Add rajma (kidney beans).
4) Now add the chopped tomatoes and cook till oil begins to float. Stir well. Also add half of the coriander leaves and half of the mint leaves with lemon juice and stir well. Cook for 2 mins till the rajma catches the flavours of the spices.
5) Wash the rice. Soak the rice for 20 mins before cooking.
6) In a cooking pot boil water till hot. Add cinnamon stick, whole cloves, whole cardamom, salt and ghee/butter or oil. Add the rice.
7) When the rice is 75% done (the rice grains begin to dance), strain it in a colander. It takes 10 -15 mins for the rice to cook at the required consistency. The rice will get completely cooked once it's layered with the prepared rajma.
8) First layer should be rajma, followed by the coriander and mint leaves and then rice. Repeat this process 2-3 times till the rice is the topmost layer. On the final layer of the rajma pulao spread the golden fried onions. Cover and cook on low heat for 10-15 mins.
9) Serve hot with raita.

RICE DISHES - VEGETARIAN

CORN PULAO
Corn Rice
(Serves approx. 4-6)

Ingredients

Sweet Corn – 1 can (341ml or 250gms)
Onions –2 medium (fried till golden brown for the layering process)
Onion – 1 big (fried till light pink)
Yogurt – ½ cup
Ginger and Garlic Paste – 1 tbsp
Red Chilly Powder – ½ tsp or as per spice level
Cinnamon Stick – 1 (3 inch)
Whole Cardamom – 4 pieces
Whole Cloves – 2 pieces
Cumin Powder (Zeera) – ½ tsp
Coriander Leaves – 1 bunch
Mint Leaves – 1 bunch
Lemon - 1 (juice of 1 lemon)
Tomatoes – 2 small (chopped)
Salt to taste
Oil
Rice – 500 gms or 2 ½ cups

Method
1) Drain the water from the sweet corn can.
2) In the oil fry 2 medium onions till golden brown and keep it aside. This will be used for the layering process.
3) Fry one big onion till light pink. Add the cinnamon stick, whole cardamom, whole cloves, red chilly powder, cumin powder, ginger and garlic paste. Stir well. Add the sweet corn
4) Now add the chopped tomatoes and cook till oil begins to float. Stir well. Also add half of the coriander leaves and half of the mint leaves with lemon juice and stir well. Cook for 2 mins till the corn catches the flavours of the spices.
5) Wash the rice. Soak the rice for 20 mins before cooking.
6) In a cooking pot boil 6 cups of water. Add cinnamon stick, whole cloves, whole cardamom, salt and ghee/butter or oil. Add the rice.
7) When the rice is 75% done (the rice grains begin to dance), strain it in a colander. It takes 10-15 mins for the rice to cook at the required consistency. The rice will get completely cooked once it's layered with the prepared sweet corn.
8) First layer should be sweet corn, followed by the coriander and mint leaves and then rice. Repeat this process 2-3 times till the rice is the topmost layer. On the final layer of the corn pulao spread the golden fried onions. Cover and cook for 10-15 mins.
9) Serve hot with raita.

RAITAS

TOMATO ONION RAITA
Tomato Onion Mixed With Yogurt

Ingredients

Onion – 1 big
Tomato – 1 big
Yogurt – 200 gms
Black Mustard Seeds – 1 tsp
Red Chilly Powder – ¼ tsp
Coriander Leaves – ½ bunch
Mint Leaves – ½ bunch (optional)
Salt to taste
Oil for tempering – 1 tbsp

Method
1) Chop the onions and tomatoes and mix well in a bowl. Add salt.
2) Whisk the yogurt and add it to the above.
3) Heat oil in a pan. Add mustard seeds and wait till the seeds crackle. Remove from the flame and add the red chilly powder immediately. Pour this into the onion and tomato mix.
4) Add the coriander leaves / mint leaves and mix well and let it cool.
5) Tomato onion raita is ready to relish.

BRINJAL RAITA
Brinjal / Aubergine Mixed With Yogurt

Ingredients

Brinjals - 1 large cut into circles
Yogurt – 200 gms
Black Mustard Seeds – 1 tsp
Red Chilly Powder – ½ tsp
Coriander Leaves – ½ bunch
Mint Leaves – ½ bunch (optional)
Salt to taste
Oil for tempering – 1 tbsp

Method
1) Cut the brinjals (aubergine) into circles. Soak them in salted water to avoid it from browning or oxidizing. Deep fry the brinjal circles. Fry till soft. Remove from the pan and place in a glass serving bowl.
2) Whisk the yogurt with salt and add it to the above.
3) Heat oil in a pan. Add mustard seeds and wait till the seeds crackle. Remove from the flame and add the red chilly powder immediately. Pour this into the brinjal mix.
4) Add the coriander leaves / mint leaves and mix well and let it cool.
5) Brinjal raita is ready to serve.

RAITAS

CUCUMBER RAITA
Cucumber Mixed With Yogurt

Ingredients

Cucumber – 1 long
Yogurt – 200 gms
Black Mustard Seeds – 1 tsp
Red Chilly Powder – ½ tsp
Coriander Leaves – ½ bunch
Mint Leaves – ½ bunch (optional)
Salt to taste
Oil for tempering – 1 tbsp

Method
1) Grate cucumber. Place in a glass serving bowl. Add salt and mix well.
2) Whisk the yogurt and add it to the above.
3) Heat oil in a pan. Add mustard seeds and wait till the seeds crackle. Remove from the flame and add the red chilly powder immediately. Pour this into the cucumber mix.
4) Add the coriander leaves / mint leaves and mix well and let it cool.
5) Cucumber raita is ready to enjoy.

ALOO KA RAITA
Potato Mixed With Yogurt

Ingredients

Onion – 1 big
Potato (Aloo) – 1 big (boiled, peeled and cubed)
Yogurt – 200 gms
Black Mustard Seeds – 1 tsp
Red Chilly Powder
Coriander Leaves – ½ bunch
Mint Leaves – ½ bunch (optional)
Salt to taste
Oil for tempering – 1 tbsp

Method
1) Chop the onions and cube the boiled potatoes and mix well in a bowl. Add salt.
2) Whisk the yogurt and add it to the above.
3) Heat oil in a pan. Add mustard seeds and wait till the seeds crackle. Remove from the flame and add the red chilly powder immediately. Pour this into the potato mix.
4) Add the coriander leaves / mint leaves and mix well and let it cool.
5) Aloo raita is ready to serve.

RAITAS

OKRA RAITA
Okra Mixed With Yogurt

Ingredients

Okra - ½ kg cut into small pieces
Yogurt – 200 gms
Black Mustard Seeds – 1 tsp
Red Chilly Powder ½ tsp
Coriander Leaves – ½ bunch
Mint Leaves – ½ bunch (optional)
Salt to taste
Oil for tempering – 1 tbsp

Method
1) Cut the okra into small pieces. Deep fry the okra. Fry till a little crisp. Remove from the pan and place in a glass serving bowl.
2) Whisk the yogurt with salt and add it to the above.
3) Heat oil in a pan. Add mustard seeds and wait till the seeds crackle. Remove from the flame and add the red chilly powder immediately. Pour this into the okra mix.
4) Add the coriander leaves / mint leaves and mix well and let it cool.
5) Okra raita is ready to relish.

BOONDI RAITA
Fried Chickpea Balls Mixed with Yogurt

Ingredients

Boondi – ½ cup
Yogurt – 200 gms
Black Mustard Seeds – 1 tsp
Red Chilly Powder – ½ tsp
Coriander Leaves – ½ bunch
Mint Leaves – ½ bunch (optional)
Salt to taste
Oil for tempering – 2 tbsp

Method
1) Place boondi in a glass serving bowl. Add salt and mix well.
2) Whisk the yogurt and add it to the above.
3) Heat oil in a pan. Add mustard seeds and wait till the seeds crackle. Remove from the flame and add the red chilly powder immediately. Pour this into the boondi mix.
4) Add the coriander leaves / mint leaves and mix well and let it cool.
5) Boondi raita is ready to serve.

DESSERTS

MAWA CUPCAKES
Indian Milk Cake
(Makes approx. 22 cupcakes)

Ingredients

Self-Raising Flour – 300 gms
Sugar – 250 gms
Butter – 250 gms
Mawa (Indian Milk Cake) – 100 gms
Eggs – 6
Baking Powder – ½ tsp
Water – ½ cup
Vanilla Essence – 1 tsp
Icing – 1 can / tube

Method
1) Whisk the butter and sugar till soft and fluffy.
2) In a separate bowl whisk the eggs with vanilla essence and water.
3) In a third bowl add the self-raising flour and baking powder and mix with light hands. Add the mawa and mix well lightly. Now add this to the eggs mixture. Slowly add butter to this mixture and make a smooth batter. Pour this into a greased baking tin.
4) Preheat the oven at 180° C (350° F).
5) Bake the mawa cake for 15-20 mins or till done.
6) Let it cool after baking. Top with desired color of icing.
7) Mawa cake is ready to relish.

STRAWBERRY CHEESECAKE
(Serves approx. 4-6)

Ingredients

Digestive Biscuits – 1 ½ cup powdered in a food processor
Condensed Milk – 1 can (225 ml)
Vanilla Essence - 1 tsp
Cream Cheese – Two 8 oz packages
Lemon Juice – ½ cup
Butter – 4 tbsp
Sugar – 2 tbsp
Strawberry Jam or Preserve – 4 tsp
Fresh Strawberries as required

Method
1) Powder the digestive biscuits finely. This will make the base of the cheese cake.
2) In a bowl add 2 tbsp of melted butter and sugar. Mix well. Now add the crushed biscuit or crackers. Mix well. In a serving dish spread this mixture to make a base for the cheesecake. Refrigerate for 15 mins.
3) Blend the condensed milk and the cream cheese. Slowly add the lemon juice and blend. Add lemon juice as per taste. Now add the strawberry preserve or jam.
4) Pour the condensed milk mixture over the refrigerated base of the cheesecake. Cover the dish with cling wrap. Refrigerate the cheesecake for 5 hours.
5) Top with fresh strawberries. Serve chilled.

DESSERTS

SHEER KORMA
Sweetened Milk with Vermicelli
(Serves approx. 6 – 8)

Ingredients

Full Cream Milk – 2 litres
Vermicelli (Seviyan) – 150 gms
Almonds – ½ cup chopped
Raisin – ¼ cup
Pistachios – ¼ cup
Sugar as per taste
Ghee (Vegetable Shortening) for frying

Method
1) Boil the full cream milk. Reduce it to 80% stirring constantly. Colour should resemble off-white or cream. Now add the sugar. Cook on low flame.
2) In a frying pan fry the chopped almonds and keep aside. Repeat the process with pistachios too. Fry the vermicelli too till it changes colour to golden brown and gives an aroma.
3) Immediately add this vermicelli to the milk and stir constantly. Add the almonds too.
4) Sheer korma is ready to serve hot. Serve the pistachios in individual bowls with sheer korma. Figs, raisins can be added too.

PINEAPPLE UPSIDE DOWN CAKE
(Serves approx. 5-7)

Ingredients

All-Purpose Flour – 300 gms
Castor Sugar – 300 gms
Butter – 150 gms
Eggs – 6
Baking Powder – 1 ½ tsp
Pineapple Essence – ½ tsp
Pineapple Slices – 1 tin
Granulated Sugar – 7 tbsp

Method
1) Preheat the oven to 180° C (350° F).
2) Grease the baking tin and spread the granulated sugar. Hold the tin over direct heat till the sugar melts and starts browning. Spread the sugar evenly.
3) Add spoonful of pineapple syrup and spread all over. Now remove from the flame. Arrange the pineapple slices and keep the tin aside.
4) In another bowl add all-purpose flour, baking powder, butter, sugar and eggs. Fold in the remaining all-purpose flour, pineapple essence and syrup. Pour into the baking tin. Bake the cake for 40 mins in the preheated oven at 180° C (350° F).
5) Cool the cake before serving. Remove the cake from the baking tin. Pineapple upside down is ready to serve.

DESSERTS

MALPUA
Sweet Indian Pancakes
(Makes approx. 8-10)

Ingredients

White Flour – 150 gms
Semolina – 40 gms
Eggs – 4
Sugar – 100 gms
Baking Powder – ¼ tsp
Mawa (Indian Milk Cake) – 100 gms
Cardamom Powder (Elaichi) – ½ tsp
Almonds – 5-6 (coarsely pound)
Fresh Cream or Maple Syrup or Honey – ½ cup
Ghee (Vegetable Shortening) for shallow frying

Method
1) Mix semolina, white flour and baking powder in a bowl. Add enough water to make it into a thick paste, then cover it and keep aside for 6-8 hrs.
2) After 8 hrs. add beaten eggs, sugar, cardamom powder, crumbled mawa, almonds and enough milk to make it into a fairly thick batter.
3) Heat ghee in a griddle or thick bottom frying pan and pour one large spoon of batter on it, covering the bottom only. Fry it until it is golden brown on one side, turn it and fry it on the other side. It should resemble a pancake.
4) Serve hot with fresh cream or maple syrup or honey.

INSTANT SAFFRON KULFI
Indian Ice-Cream flavoured with Saffron
(Serves approx. 3-5)

Ingredients

Condensed Milk – 1 tin (225 ml)
Cream – 2 small tins (170 gms each tin)
Full Cream Milk – 250 ml
Saffron (Kesar) Strands – 9 or 10
Almonds – 2 tbsp chopped
Pistachios – 1 tbsp chopped

Method
1) In a bowl add condensed milk, cream and full cream milk. Whisk this mixture.
2) In a small bowl soak the saffron strands in 4 tbsp of milk. Add this to the condensed milk mixture. Whisk well. Add the almonds and pistachios as garnish.
3) Pour this mixture in a freezer proof serving bowl. Freeze for 4–5 hrs.
4) Let the frozen kulfi stand for 5 mins before serving.

GLOSSARY

INDIAN NAME	ENGLISH NAME
Aloo	Potato
Arhar Dal	Spilt Red Lentil
Ajwain	Carom Seeds
Adrak	Ginger
Ananas	Pineapple
Andaa	Egg
Badam	Almond
Bhajia	Fritters
Bhagaar	Tempering
Baingan	Brinjals / Aubergines
Brishta	Fried Onion Slices
Biryani	Rice flavoured with spices
Boondi	Fried Chickpea Balls
Bhendi	Okra / Ladyfinger
Bhutta	Corn
Besan	Chickpea Powder
Chana	Chickpea
Chana Dal	Bengal Gram Lentil
Cheeni	Sugar
Chukandar	Beetroot
Dal	Lentil
Dalchini	Cinnamon
Dahi	Yogurt
Dhania	Coriander
Doodh	Milk
Elaichi	Cardamom
Ghee	Clarified Butter
Garam Masala	All Spices
Gajar	Carrot
Gobi	Cabbage
Gosht	Meat
Hara	Green
Hari Mirchi	Green Chilly
Haldi	Turmeric
Imli	Tamarind

INDIAN NAME	ENGLISH NAME
Jaiphal	Nutmeg
Javitri	Mace
Jhingah	Prawns / Shrimps
Kali Mirchi	Pepper
Kebab	Cutlet
Kacche	Raw
Kheema	Mince Meat
Kaju	Cashewnut
Kofta	Meatball
Khada Masala	Whole Spices
Kishmish	Raisin
Kesar	Saffron
Korma	Gravy
Khoya	Indian Milk Cake
Kulfi	Indian Ice-Cream
Kotmir	Coriander Leaves
Laung	Cloves
Lal Mirchi	Red Chilly
Lehsun	Garlic
Mawa	Indian Milk Cake
Masala	Mixture of spices
Makhani	Mix of butter, tomatoes and cream
Makhan	Butter
Malpua	Sweet Indian Pancake
Maida	All Purpose Flour
Methi	Fenugreek
Murg	Chicken
Moong Dal	Spilt Green Gram Lentil
Masoor Dal	Split Red Lentil
Machhli	Fish
Mooli	Radish
Mutter	Peas
Nariyal	Coconut
Nimbu	Lemon
Naan	Indian Bread

GLOSSARY & KITCHEN CONVERSION TABLE

INDIAN NAME	ENGLISH NAME
Paani	Water
Pakoda	Dumpling
Phool Gobi	Cauliflower
Pyaaz	Onion
Pudina	Mint Leaves
Paaya	Trotters
Palak	Spinach
Paneer	Cottage Cheese
Pista	Pistachios
Pulao	Rice flavoured with few spices
Qubooli / Chana	Split Yellow Lentil
Raita	Yogurt Dip made with vegetables or fruit
Roti	Indian Bread
Rava	Semolina
Rai	Mustard Seeds
Rajma	Red Kidney Beans
Suji	Semolina
Seviyan	Vermicelli
Sheer	Milk
Shakkar	Sugar
Shishumul	Arrowroot
Shimla Mirch	Capsicum
Sabzee	Vegetable
Salan	Gravy
Saunf	Fennel Seed
Tejpatta	Bayleaf
Tuvar Dal	Split Red Gram Lentil
Urad Dal	Split Black Gram Lentil
Vada	Dumpling
Zeera	Cumin
Zaffran	Saffron

KITCHEN CONVERSION TABLE

1 gram = .035 ounce
100 grams = 3.5 ounces
500 grams = 1.10 pounds
1 kilogram = 2.205 pounds
1 kilogram = 35 oz
1 oz. = 28 grams
1 pound = 454 grams
1/4 Cup = 12 tsp = 4 tbsp
1 Cup = 48 tsp = 16 tbsp

NOTES

www.ingramcontent.com/pod-product-compliance
Lightning Source LLC
Chambersburg PA
CBHW061930290426
44113CB00024B/2862